AF600500

THE CATHOLIC UNIVERSITY OF AMERICA
CANON LAW STUDIES
No. 227

The "ab acatholicis nati" of Canon 1099, § 2

A HISTORICAL SYNOPSIS AND COMMENTARY

BY
REV. WARREN L. BOUDREAUX, J.C.L.
Priest of the Diocese of Lafayette (Louisiana)

A DISSERTATION

Submitted to the Faculty of the School of Canon Law of the Catholic University of America in Partial Fulfillment of the Requirements for the Degree of Doctor of Canon Law

THE CATHOLIC UNIVERSITY OF AMERICA PRESS
WASHINGTON, D. C.
1946

Nihil Obstat:

Ludovicus Motry, S.T.D., J.C.D.,

Censor Deputatus.

Washingtonii, D. C., May 31, 1947.

Imprimatur:

✠ Julius Benjamin Jeanmard, D.D., LL.D.,

Episcopus Lafayettensis.

Lafayettensi, Louisiana, die 2 junii, 1947.

Printed by
The Paulist Press
401 West 59th Street
New York 19, N. Y.

51

TO

HIS EXCELLENCY

THE MOST REVEREND JULES B. JEANMARD, D.D., LL.D.

ASSISTANT AT THE PONTIFICAL THRONE

TABLE OF CONTENTS

PART II

CANONICAL COMMENTARY

CHAPTER IV

CHAPTER V

CHAPTER VI

CHAPTER VII

CHAPTER VIII

CHAPTER IX

INTRODUCTION

THE Canonical problems that arise in parochial work and in the diocesan tribunals of America are becoming increasingly more frequent and varied. None of them, however, is so much in evidence as that which has its origin in marriage legislation, and especially regarding the obligation to the canonical form. This is due in large measure to the non-Catholic environment existing in the United States and the steadily increasing number of mixed marriages throughout the country.

Of particular interest and intricacy are those problems which arise from the exemption from the canonical form allowed in canon 1099, § 2. The first paragraph of the canon is comparatively clear. It states that there are held to the canonical form of marriage all those who have been baptized in the Catholic Church. These are always bound to observe the form, even though they later defected from the Church.[1] They are bound, moreover, not only when they contract marriage among themselves, but also when they contract marriage with non-Catholics, whether baptized or not, and even after a dispensation has been obtained from the impediment of mixed religion or disparity of cult.[2] The fact that one party of the marriage is bound to the Catholic form obliges also the other to the form, even though the latter is otherwise free from the obligation. The Code of Canon Law abrogated the principle of the shared exemption in its entirety. An individual who is once bound to the canonical form is bound to it always, and in marrying one who is not directly subject to the observance of the Church's juridical form, he communicates his own obligation to that person. Hence non-Catholics are indirectly held to the canonical form. The same is true of Orientals who contract marriage with Latins who are themselves bound.[3]

Non-Catholics, however, whether baptized or not, are never

[1] Canon 1099, I, n. 1.

[2] *Ibidem,* n. 2.

[3] *Ibidem,* n. 3.

bound to the Catholic form when they marry among themselves. In so far as the Church does not legislate for the non-baptized, infidels are outside the binding force of the canonical form.[4] While baptized non-Catholics are held by ecclesiastical laws unless they are expressly exempted,[5] there is an express exemption which frees them from the obligation of submitting themselves to the Catholic form of marriage provided they marry among themselves.[6] This presumes, however, that such non-Catholics were baptized outside the Catholic Church in heresy or schism and were never converted; for all those who were baptized in the Catholic Church, or who, though baptized as non-Catholics, were subsequently converted to the Catholic Church, are always bound to the observance of the form. There is one exception to this general rule. It is this exception which constitutes the subject matter of this dissertation.

The exemption allowed to non-Catholics is clear and is an application of the general rule that only those who have been baptized in the Catholic Church or converted to it are bound to marry according to the norms determined in the Code,[7] but the second paragraph of canon 1099 then states that there are also others who are excused from the form of marriage; namely, all those who are born of non-Catholics, even though they were baptized in the Catholic Church, and who grew up from infancy in heresy or schism, or in infidelity, or without any religion. These are not held to the canonical form of marriage if they contract marriage with non-Catholics. In the language of the canon they also are exempted from the form who are "ab acatholicis nati, etsi in Ecclesia Catholica baptizati, qui ab infantili aetate in haeresi vel schismate aut infidelitate vel sine ulla religione adoleverunt, quoties cum parte acatholica contraxerint." It is in this part of the canon that difficulties of interpretation can arise. To begin with, it is a new provision of the general ecclesiastical law

[4] Canon 12. Cf. Payen, *De Matrimonio in Missionibus ac Potissimum in Sinis, Tractatus Practicus et Casus* (editio altera, 3 vols. Zi-ka-wei: Typographia T'ou-sè-wè, 1935-1936), II, n. 1843 (hereafter referred to as *De Matrimonio*); canon 1099, § 2.

[5] Canon 87.

[6] Canon 1099, § 2.

[7] Canon 1099, § 1.

and is a startling exception to the general principle that all those who are baptized in the Catholic Church are held to the Catholic form of marriage. Many, moreover, consider it only tentative legislation that has not yet stood the test of time. Authors in attempting to explain the canon have disagreed on many important points, and have avoided others almost entirely, so that practical cases involving the principle have become a source of distress to pastors and ecclesiastical tribunals.

The present work endeavors to give a canonical commentary on this paragraph of canon 1099 and on the conditions required as there determined to induce the exemption from the observance of the form of marriage. The first part of the work presents a brief historical outline of the law on the form of marriage. The second part constitutes a canonical commentary which treats of each condition as determined in the law, and offers further considerations regarding the obligation of the *"ab acatholicis nati"* to other Church laws.

It is needless to say that doctrinal elucidations on this particular subject are quite meager. Many authors are satisfied merely to paraphrase the canon and to refer to those answers of the Pontifical Commission for the Authentic Interpretation of the Code that have settled disputed points; others who treat the subject more completely show signs of uncertainty in the opinions they propose.

The writer wishes to express his sincere gratitude to His Excellency, the Most Reverend Jules B. Jeanmard, D.D., Bishop of Lafayette, Louisiana, for the opportunity afforded him for graduate study; to the members of the Faculty of the School of Canon Law for their kind assistance and guidance in the preparation of this work; to his fellow students for their generous assistance, and to his family and friends for their constant encouragement.

Part I

Historical Synopsis

CHAPTER I

TRIDENTINE LEGISLATION AND THE DECREE *Tametsi*

Article 1. The Adoption of the Decree *Tametsi*

The twenty-fourth session of the Council of Trent, the eighth under Pope Pius IV (1559-1565), was convoked on November 11, 1563. In accordance with the vote on the preceding day, the canons on matrimony and the decree on clandestine marriages were proposed for final adoption as the legislation of the Church. The canons and the decree were read to the assembled Fathers, then the votes were gathered individually by the Secretary of the Council, Bishop Massarelli (1510-1566), and two other notaries. The vote was substantially the same as that which had been received throughout the long preliminary discussions. Fifty-six of the Fathers voted against the decree, one hundred and thirty-five supported it, and nine either remitted themselves to the judgment of the Holy See in the matter or refrained from voicing a definite opinion.[1] Cardinal Charles of Lorraine (de Guise), Archbishop of Rheims (1538-1574), and Cardinal Louis Madruzzo of Trent, both of them leaders in all the previous discussion on the question, cast their traditional vote, the former approving and the latter opposing the decree. Even the four papal legates to the Council were divided. While John Cardinal Morone

[1] Ehses (1855-1926) stated that 55 Fathers opposed the decree, but he did not seem to be counting in that number the Cardinal Hosius of Warmia, who was ill at the time and did not cast his opposing vote till later.—*Concilii Tridentini Diariorum, Actorum, Epistularum, Tractuum Nova Collectio* (13 vols., Friburgi Brisgoviae: Herder, 1901-1938), Vol. IX (ed. S. Ehses, 1924), 977 (hereafter referred to as Ehses); Theiner, *Acta Genuina SS. Oecumenici Concilii Tridentini* (2 vols., Zagabriae, Croatia, 1874), II, 232 (hereafter cited as Theiner).

and Bernardine Cardinal Navagero voted in favor of the decree, Cardinal Simonetta and Cardinal Hosius opposed it, but submitted themselves to the Holy See, as did many of the opposing faction. With such division among the leaders of the Council, some thought the decree should not be enacted; but on January 26, 1564, all the decrees of the Council of Trent were confirmed by a Bull of the Pope. The decree *Tametsi* definitely became law.[2]

Article 2. Legislation of the Decree.[3]

The legislation of the Decree adopted by the Council reads as follows: Though it is not to be doubted that clandestine marriages made with the free consent of the contracting parties are valid and true marriages so long as the Church has not made them invalid,[4] and therefore they are rightly to be condemned, as the holy synod does condemn with anathema those who deny that they are true and valid, as also those who falsely say that marriages contracted by children without the consent of their parents are invalid, or that parents can make them valid or invalid,[5] nevertheless the holy Church of God has for most just reason always detested and forbidden them.[6]

[2] Pius IV, "*Bulla Confirmationis Concilii,*" 26 ian. 1564—Ehses, p. 1150. For list of arguments and notes of Fathers, cf. Ehses, pp. 971-977. For list of Fathers at the eighth session, cf. Ehses, pp. 1004-1007.

[3] Ehses, p. 968; Le Plat, *Canones et Decreta Sacrosancti Oecumenici et Generalis Concilii Tridentini* (Antwerpiae: Plantin, 1779), p. 247 (hereafter referred to as Le Plat). This latter work was officially edited at Rome in 1564; then, after many reprints, by Le Plat in 1779; finally, at Rome by the Polyglot Press in 1904.

[4] The fourth draft had: "Quamdiu ecclesia irrita non fecit."—Ehses, p. 889. The session had: "Quamdiu ecclesia ea irrita non fecit."—Ehses, p. 968. Cf. c. 2, X, *de clandestina desponsatione*, IV, 3. The references of this historical section are taken from the traditional footnotes of the editions following Chifflet (1597-1657). Philippe Chifflet's edition of the *Canones et Decreta Concilii Tridentini* was published at Antwerp in 1640.

[5] The phrase "or that parents can make them valid or invalid" is not included in Schroeder's translation of the Decree.—Schroeder, *Canons and Decrees of the Council of Trent* (St. Louis: Herder, 1941), p. 183. Though the writer has followed the translation of Schroeder, he has felt free to differ occasionally.

[6] In the famous decree "Aliter" (c. I, C. XXX, q. 5) clandestine marriages

But since the Holy Synod recognizes that these prohibitions are of no effect because of the disobedience of men, and weighs the grave sins that arise from these clandestine marriages, especially the sins of those who remain in the state of damnation, when, having abandoned the first wife with whom they have contracted secretly,[7] they publicly contract with another and live with her in continual adultery, which evil[8] the Church, which does not judge what is hidden, cannot correct unless some more efficacious remedy is used, therefore, following the lead of the Holy Lateran Council celebrated under Innocent III[9] commands that in the future before a marriage is contracted, there shall be publicly announced, three times in Church by the proper pastor of the contracting parties during the celebration of Mass on three successive festival days, the names of those persons between whom the marriage is to be contracted; after which publications, if no impediment is revealed, the marriage may be proceeded with publicly in the church (*in facie ecclesiae*), where the pastor, having questioned the man and woman and having accepted their mutual consent,[10] shall say, "I join you together in matrimony, in the name of the Father, and of the Son, and of the Holy Ghost," or shall use other words according to the accepted rite of each province. But if at times there should be a probable

are forbidden. The canon, however, is spurious and must be attributed to Pseudo-Isidore. Cf. Le Plat, p. 248. Cf. also C. 3, C. XXX, q. 5.

[7] The fourth draft had: "cum qua clam *contraxerunt.*"—Ehses, p. 889; Theiner, II, 425.

The draft accepted by the session had "cum qua clam *contraxerant.*"—Ehses, p. 968; Le Plat, p. 247.

[8] The decree *"Non Omnis"* (C. 12, C. XXXII, q. 2) clarified the distinction between *uxor* and *concubina,* and warned parents to give their daughters in legitimate marriages.

[9] C. 3, X, *de clandestina desponsatione,* IV, 3; c. 51, X, *de clandestina desponsatione,* IV, 3. The Council required public announcement of all marriages in order to facilitate the detection of possible impediments, and withdrew the beneficial status of a putative marriage from all clandestine marriages contracted with a diriment impediment.

[10] The fourth draft had only "viro et muliere interrogatis."—Ehses, p. 899; Theiner, II, 425.

The session draft had "viro et muliere interrogatis et eorum mutuo consensu intellecto."—Ehses, p. 968; Le Plat, p. 247.

suspicion that a marriage might be maliciously interfered with if so many announcements precede it, then either only one announcement may be permitted, or the marriage may be celebrated forthwith in the presence of at least the pastor and two or three witnesses; then, before its consummation, the announcements shall be made in church in order that if any impediments exist they may be more easily detected, unless the ordinary himself shall decide it expedient that the above-mentioned announcements shall be omitted.[11] which the Holy Synod leaves to his prudence and judgment. Whoever shall attempt [12] to contract marriage otherwise than in the presence of the pastor or of some other priest with the permission of the pastor or of the ordinary, and also in the presence of two or three witnesses, the Holy Synod renders them wholly incapable of so contracting, and decrees that such contracts are invalid and null, as by the present decree it invalidates and annuls them. Moreover, it commands that the pastor or another priest who shall have been present at a contract of this kind [13] with a smaller number of witnesses, and the witnesses so present without the pastor or another priest, as well as the contracting parties themselves, shall be gravely punished according to the discretion of the ordinary. Furthermore the same Holy Synod exhorts the betrothed parties not to live together in the same house before having received the sacerdotal blessing in the church,[14] and it decrees that the blessing is to be given by the proper pastor, and that the permission to give the above-mentioned blessing cannot be

[11] The fourth draft had "ut praedictae solemnitates remittantur."—Ehses, p. 889; Theiner, II, 425.

The session form had "ut praedictae denuntiationes remittantur."—Ehses, p. 968; Le Plat, p. 247.

[12] The fourth draft had "qui aliter . . . attentaverit."—Ehses, p. 889.

The session form had: "qui aliter attentabunt."—Ehses, p. 968; Le Plat, p. 247.

[13] The fourth draft had "Matrimonio interfuerint."—Ehses, p. 889; Theiner, II, 425.

The session form had: "huiusmodi contractui interfuerint."—Ehses, p. 968; Le Plat, p. 247.

[14] This sacerdotal blessing had long been required by law.—c. 2, C. XXX, q. 5.

conceded to another priest except by the pastor himself or by the ordinary, any contrary custom whatsoever, even immemorial, which is rather to be called an abuse or also any privilege to the contrary notwithstanding. But if any pastor or any other priest, whether he be a regular or a secular, shall dare to unite in marriage or bless the betrothed parties of another parish without the permission of the pastor,[15] even though he claim the right for himself because of a privilege or immemorial custom, he shall remain *ipso iure* suspended until he is absolved by the ordinary of the pastor who ought to have been present at the marriage, or from whom the blessing ought to have been received. The pastor shall have a book, which he shall carefully guard, in which he shall record the names of the betrothed parties and of the witnesses, and also the date when and the place where the marriage was contracted. Lastly, the Holy Synod exhorts the betrothed parties that before they contract marriage or at least three days before its consummation, they diligently confess their sins and piously approach the most holy sacrament of the Eucharist. If any provinces have in this matter laudable customs and ceremonies beyond the above-mentioned, the Holy Synod most earnestly wishes that they be retained. Lest these salutary precepts remain unknown to anyone, it commands all ordinaries that, as soon as they possibly can,[16] they take care that this decree be published and explained to the people in all parochial churches of their dioceses, and that this be done very often during the first year, and after that as often as they shall deem it advisable. It further orders that this decree shall begin to take effect in each parish at the expiration of thirty days, to be reckoned from the day of its first publication in that parish.

[15] In the session form (Ehses, p. 968) it reads: "sine illorum parochi licentia." Le Plat has: "sine illorum parochiae licentia."

[16] The fourth draft had: "ut quamprimum potuerint."—The session had: "ut cum primum potuerint."—Ehses, p. 968.

Yet in the draft adopted by the session according to Le Plat (p. 247) the "ut quamprimum potuerint" is used.

CHAPTER II

POST-TRIDENTINE LEGISLATION

ARTICLE 1. THE DECREE *Tamesti* AND ITS APPLICATION

THE decree on marriage, it has been seen, bound all baptized persons to observe the juridical form enacted by the Fathers of the Council of Trent; but the decree did not immediately affect the whole world. It had been decided by the Council that the law was to be binding only in those parishes in which it was promulgated. This promulgation devolved upon each ordinary and the decree itself, in determining this promulgation, had established that the decree was to have the force of law only thirty (30) days after its promulgation in each parish.[1] It was both intended and expected that the decree should be published throughout the world; but such was not the case. It was never published in several countries but such was not the result intended. In other countries it was published only within certain districts.[2]

Since clandestine marriages were therefore still valid in those regions where the decree *Tametsi* had not been published, the decree failed in much of its intended purpose.[3]

Where the decree had been published, however, clandestine marriages entered into without the Tridentine form were invalid.[4] The

[1] *Canones et Decreta Sacrosancti Oecumenici Concilii Tridentini sub Paulo III, Julio III, et Pio VI Pontificibus Maximis,* editio stereotypa (Ratisbonae, 1903), p. 205; Conc. Trident., sess. xxiv, *de ref. matrim.*, c. 1.

[2] For places of publication cf. Wernz, Franciscus X, Ius Decretalium (6 vols., Romae et Prati, 1898-1905, Vol. IV, Romae, 1904), IV, 237-244.

[3] S. C. Concilii, 18 ian. 1663 (ad Ep. Tricarien.)—*Collectanea S. Congregationis de Propaganda Fide* (2 vols., Romae: Typographia Polyglotta S. C. de Propaganda Fide, 1907), n. 149. This collection is hereafter referred to as *Coll. S.C.P.F.*

[4] S. C. de Prop. Fide (C. P. pro. Sin. Tunkin. Occid.), 5 apr. 1785—*Codicis Iuris Canonici Fontes cura Emi. Petri Card. Gasparri editi* (9 vols., Romae: Typis Polyglottis Vaticanis, 1923-1939. Vols. VII, VIII, IX, ed. cura et studio Emi. Iustiniani Card. Seredi) n. 4601. This work is hereafter referred to as *Fontes.*

desired peace that had long been intended by the Council of Trent resulted in confusion, and the strong safeguards that had been placed around the dignity and sanctity of the sacrament of marriage again failed to achieve their contemplated purpose. This was true of Catholics. It was true especially in relation to heretics and schismatics.

In principle, heretics and schismatics were also bound to observe the form enacted by the decree *Tametsi,* for as baptized persons they came within the pale of the Church's legislative jurisdiction.[5]

Yet with the spread of heresy becoming more rapid and extensive, and with Catholicism being prescribed in some places, the Holy See realized that, unless some exemptions were granted to heretics, numberless invalid marriages would arise. Wherefore, the following policy was, in general, adopted:

1. In regions where *Tametsi* was never published, marriages of heretics, contracted without the prescribed form, were valid.[6]

2. Where Catholicism prevailed and *Tametsi* was in force, and where heretics comprised but a minority, such heretics were bound.[7]

3. Where heretical religions were formed into distinct organizations, with their own ministers, such heretics were not bound, since in such cases the decree *Tametsi* was adjudged to be extended only to Catholics.[8]

As practical problems developed, and accordingly demanded a

[5] Conc. Trident., sess. VII, de baptismo C. 7: "If anyone saith that the baptized are, by baptism itself, made debtors to faith alone, and not to the observance of the whole law of Christ; let him be anathema."

CC. 8: "If anyone saith that the baptized are freed from all the precepts, whether written or transmitted, of holy Church, in such wise that they are not bound to observe them, unless they have chosen of their own accord to submit themselves thereunto, let him be anathema.—Conc. Trident., sess. VII, *de bapt.;* Waterworth, *The Canons and Decrees of the Sacred and Oecumenical Council of Trent* (London: C. Dolman, 1848), p. 56.

[6] S. C. Conc., 18 ian. 1663 (ad *Ep. Tricarien.)—Coll. S.C.P.F.,* n. 149.

[7] S. C. C., 18 ian. 1663 (ad *Ep. Tricarien.)—Coll. S.C.P.F.,* n. 149; *Acta Sanctae Sedis* (41 vols., Romae, 1865-1908), XXXII (1898), 407 (hereafter referred to as *ASS*).

[8] S. C. C., declar. *Matrimonia,* 4 nov. 1741—*Fontes,* n. 3527; Pius X, litt. ap. *Provida,* 18 ian. 1906—*ASS,* XXXIX (1906-1907), 81; Wernz, *Ius Decretalium,* IV, 246-256.

solution, it was further decided that the decree lost its binding force through a protracted period of non-application, just as it could and did acquire a binding force through a long period of official application even without the prescribed form of promulgation.[9]

Moreover if one party to the marriage was free from the observance of the form of marriage as required by the Council of Trent, he communicated that exemption to the other party, and thus the contractants of the marriage were not subjected to the decree *Tametsi*.[10]

The declaration of Pope Bendict XIV (1740-1758) in stating that marriages between heretics and Catholics were valid even though entered upon without the form prescribed by the Council of Trent was directed to Holland, but was extended to Germany and other regions where non-Catholics were present in preponderant numbers.[11]

Article 2. The Decree *Tametsi* and Those Baptized Catholics Exempt from Its Obligation

In the jurisprudence developed in relation to the decree *Tametsi*, there is found something very pertinent to the status of persons baptized in the Catholic Church but who were not brought up as Catholics. In 1859 the Sacred Congregation of the Holy Office issued a response to the Bishop of Haarlem, in Holland.[12] The Holy Office in relation to the Benedictine Declaration included under the name of heretics the five following classes:

[9] S. C. C., Poloniae, 13 nov. 1638—*Fontes*, 2594; Cf. Wernz, *Ius Decretalium*, IV., n. 160.

[10] S. C. C., declar. *Matrimonii*, 4 nov. 1741—*Fontes*, n. 3537. Cf. Wernz, *op. cit.*, IV, n. 173; S. C. S. Off., (inst. ad Arch. *Quebecen.*) 16 sept. 1824—*Fontes*, n. 866.

[11] S. C. C., declar. *Matrimonii*, 4 nov. 1741—*Fontes*, n. 3527; Pius X, litt. ap. *Provida*, 18 ian., 1906—*ASS*, XXXIX (1906-1907), 81—*Fontes*, n. 670. For a discussion whether the so called Benedictine declaration implied an extended exemption from the law, or a mere declaration of an exemption already in force, as well as for a list of the places determined as affected by the Apostolic Letter *Provida*, cf. Wernz, *Ius Decretalium*, IV, n. 163. Cf. Benedictus XIV, *De Synodo Dioecesana* (Parmae, 1764), lib. VI, cap. VI.

[12] S. C. S. Off., litt. (*ad Ep. Harlemen.*), 6 apr. 1859—*Fontes* 950; *Coll. S.C.P.F.*, n. 1174.

1. Persons baptized in the Catholic Church, but who were reared in heresy or who professed heresy from earliest childhood and onward (*a pueritia nondum septennali*).

2. Persons baptized in the Catholic Church, but educated by heretics, even though they had received little education in heresy, and though they had not been consistently active in heresy or heretical sects.

3. Persons baptized in the Catholic Church who in childhood had fallen under the influence of heretics, and then had joined a heretical sect.

4. Apostates from the Catholic Church who had gone over to heretical sects.

5. Persons born of heretics and baptized by heretics, even though they had never professed loyalty to any heretical sect or to any religion.

The decree *Tametsi* was not to be applicable as law for these five groups; and the Catholic parties who had entered marriage with any persons belonging to one or the other of these groups were not to be disturbed, even though such marriage had been contracted without the canonical form.

Thus the Holy Office decided that in Holland, under the Benedictine Declaration, the marriages of persons baptized in the Catholic Church educated in heresy or professing heresy from earliest childhood onward (*a pueritia nondum septennali*) were not bound by the prescriptions of the decree *Tametsi.* In the same juridical position were all those who had been educated by heretics, even though they were not consistently active in heretical sects, all apostates, all children (*pueri*) who had joined heretical sects, all who were baptized in heresy and all those who had grown up without any religion.

CHAPTER III

THE DECREE *NE TEMERE*

ARTICLE 1. THE GENERAL APPLICATION OF THE DECREE *Ne temere*

THE decree *Ne temere* became law on Easter Sunday, April 19, 1908.[1] According to the norms of the decree all Catholics of the Latin rite, when marrying among themselves, were bound to enter marriage before two witnesses and either the parish priest of the place, or the ordinary of the place, where the marriage was performed, or a priest delegated by either. Catholics were also bound to this form when they married non-Catholics, baptized or unbaptized, unless a dispensation had been granted by the Holy See. Orientals were, in general, not bound by the requirements of the decree *Ne temere*, since it applied to the faithful of the Latin rite. Orientals were bound, however, whenever they contracted marriage with Latins, to follow the Latin form as required in *Ne temere*.[2] To this general rule an exception was made for Greek Ruthenians in Galicia, in the United States of America, in Canada, and in South America who were subjected to the provisions of *Ne temere*.[3]

In general, too, the decree *Ne temere* abolished the Benedictine Declaration in all its extensions. It removed the communication of exemption whereby a party who was not bound to the Catholic form could communicate this freedom to one who was otherwise bound to the form. An exception obtained in Germany, however,

[1] S. C. C., decr. *Ne temere*, 2 aug. 1907—*Fontes*, n. 4340, *ASS*, XL (1907-1908), 525-530.

[2] S. C. C., *Romana et Aliarum*, 1 febr. 1908, ad I et III—*Fontes*, n. 4344; S. C. C., *Romana et Aliarum*, 28 mart. 1908, ad I—*Fontes*, n. 4349.

[3] S. C. de Prop. Fide pro negotiis Ritus Orientalis, 21, maii, 1911—*Archiv fur katholisches Kirchenrecht*, (Innsbruck, 1857-1861; Mainz 1862—), XCII (1911), 484; this work will hereafter be referred to as *A.K.K.R.* S. C. de Prop. Fide pro negotiis Ritus Orientalis, 19 aug. 1913, art. 36—*Acta Apostolicae Sedis, Commentarium Officiale* (Romae, 1909—), V (1913), 398. This work is hereafter referred to as *AAS*, VI (1914), 463; *AAS*, VIII (1916), 107.

where the extensions granted in 1906 were retained according to the special law of the Apostolic Letter *Provida;* the same was true of Hungary.[4] Other then these exemptions the binding force of the decree *Ne temere* on one party sufficed to obligate both parties of the marriage to the form which this decree prescribed.

ARTICLE 2. THE DECREE *Ne temere* AND THOSE BORN OF NON-CATHOLICS

Even where the exemptions from *Ne temere* existed, however, the application of the law for those who were not bound to the form, and who were able to communicate their exemption to the other party who was bound when the two married, no longer remained what it had been in the response of the Holy Office to the Bishop of Haarlem.[5] In that response, the Holy Office had included under the name of heretics who shared the extension of the Benedictine Declaration, namely, the power in the act of contracting marriage to communicate their freedom from the law to another who was bound to the form, all persons baptized in the Catholic Church but educated in or professing heresy from earliest childhood onward. It included as well all baptized children, even those baptized in the Catholic Church, who had later become members of heretical sects or who had apostatized.

These, however, were not included after the promulgation of *Ne temere,* even where the extensions of the Benedictine Declaration were retained. In a response to Germany, where by special law clandestine mixed marriages were still recognized as valid, the Sacred Congregation of the Council in 1908 declared that even those who from juvenile or infant age had fallen from the faith were held to the form of the decree *Ne temere* when they married a Catholic party, and that this ruling touched the validity of the marriage.[6]

This seemed to indicate just who were to be considered Catholics in respect of the obligation to observe the form prescribed by the

[4] Pius X, litt. ap. *Provida,* 18 ian. 1906—*ASS,* XXXIX (1906), 81; *Fontes,* n. 670; S. C. C, *Romana et Aliarum,* 1 febr. 1908, ad. IV—*Fontes,* n. 4344; S. C. C. *Romana et Aliarum,* 28 mart. 1908, ad. III—*Fontes,* n. 4349; S. C. de Sacram., 27 febr. 1909—*A.K.K.R.,* LXXIX (1909), 717-724.

[5] S. C. C. Off., litt. (ad Ep. Harlemen.), 6 apr. 1859—*Fontes,* n. 950.

[6] S. C. C., *Romana et Aliarum,* 1 febr. 1908, ad V et VI—*Fontes,* n. 4344.

decree *Ne temere;* and it seemed to include in that number those who previously had been considered under the name of heretics in the response given to the Bishop of Haarlem, including children baptized in the Catholic faith, but reared from childhood in heresy. The implication, however, was not completely clear. It was true, of course, that the decree *Ne temere* itself exempted only non-Catholics from the form, and the answer of the Sacred Congregation of the Council on February 1, 1908, did seem to include persons baptized in the Catholic Church but reared from infancy in heresy as being held to the form, but it did so only in the express event that they married Catholics.

Since in Germany non-Catholics by special law could still communicate their exemption from the form to Catholics even after the promulgation of *Ne temere,* and since the answer of the Sacred Congregation of the Council expressly stated that persons baptized in the Catholic Church but reared from infancy in heresy were bound to the form when they married Catholics, it seemed clear enough that the latter possessed no exemption which they could communicate, in opposition to that which non-Catholics did possess in Germany, and that therefore they were to be considered, not as non-Catholics but as Catholics who themselves were bound to observe the Catholic form. It was the common teaching that once one had been a member of the Church even by baptism alone, one was held to observe the canonical form of marriage prescribed by the decree *Ne temere.*[7] However, on March 31, 1911, the Sacred Congregation of the Holy Office decreed that recourse was required to be made to the Holy See in each case whenever a question arose regarding the validity of a marriage contracted with a non-Catholic or with an infidel on the part of one who was born of non-Catholic or infidel parents, but after Catholic baptism, grew up from infancy onward either in heresy, or in infidelity, or without any religion whatsoever.[8]

[7] Wernz, *Ius Decretalium,* IV, n. 188; Schaaf, "Exemption of the *'ab acatholicis nati'* under the decree *'Ne temere'*", *The Ecclesiastical Review* (Philadelphia, 1889-1944; Washington, D. C., 1944-), XCIV (1936), 188-189; Allen, "The Test of Catholicity of Canon 1099, 2"—*The Jurist,* (Washington, D. C., 1941-), III (1943), 598.

[8] *ASS,* III (1911), 163-164.

Part II

Canonical Commentary

CHAPTER IV

THE "*AB ACATHOLICIS NATI*" IN THE LAW OF THE CODE

(CANON 1099, § 1, 1°-2°)

Article 1. The New Law

The Code of Canon Law went into effect on May 19, 1918. Relative to the form of marriage with respect to those persons who were bound to observe the form the present law does not differ essentially from the prescriptions of *Ne temere.* All Catholics of the Latin rite, whether baptized in the Catholic Church or converted to it from heresy or schism, are bound to observe the Catholic form of marriage whenever they marry among themselves or even when they marry non-Catholics. This obligation of the observance of the canonical form does not lapse even though the baptized Catholics or the converts to the Catholic Church defect from the Church, and even though the necessary dispensation to marry a non-Catholic, when such is the case, has been acquired.[1] Orientals, when marrying among themselves, are not affected by the Code; but they are held to the Latin form of marriage whenever they marry members of the Latin Rite.[2] Non-Catholics, baptized or unbaptized, when marrying among themselves are in no way bound to the canonical form of marriage.[3]

This is essentially the same legislation that had been in force under the decree *Ne temere.*[4] There is, however, an element in the new legislation of the Code that had not found any place in the

[1] Canon 1099, § 1, nn. 1-2.

[2] Canon 1099, § 1, n. 3.

[3] Canon 1099, § 2.

[4] S. C. C., decr. *Ne temere,* 2 aug. 1907—*Fontes,* n. 4340.

decree *Ne temere.* According to the present law, persons born of non-Catholics (*"ab acatholicis nati"*), even though baptized in the Catholic Church, who from infancy (*ab infantili aetate*) grew up in heresy, or schism, or infidelity, or without any religion at all, are not bound to observe the Catholic form of marriage whenever they contract marriage with non-Catholics.[5] The notion, however, of this exemption is not entirely new. As previously indicated, in a response of the Holy Office to the Bishop of Haarlem in Holland, the class of persons baptized in the Catholic Church but reared from infancy in heresy was considered as heretical and as not subject to the Tridentine legislation on the canonical form of marriage, and was declared to share the extension of the Benedictine Declaration.[6] Though the decree *Ne temere* had revoked the exemption of this class, still the Holy Office declared in 1911 that in each case of a marriage contracted by a non-Catholic or by an infidel with a person born of non-Catholics but baptized in the Catholic Church and reared from infancy outside of the Church recourse was to be had to the Holy See when the validity of such a marriage was to be determined upon the issue of the obligation to observe the form of the marriage contract.[7] Now, as a result of the present legislation, the class of persons born of non-Catholics (*"ab acatholicis nati"*) who are reared from infancy outside of the Catholic Church are by law exempted from the Catholic form of marriage whenever they marry non-Catholics.

Article 2. The First Response of the Pontifical Commission for the Interpretation of the Code

The early commentators of the Code, in treating of the form of marriage and of the persons bound to observe it, often did little more than state in their own words the legislation of the Code, without further commentary on the meaning of the terms. A number of authors, therefore, did not treat of the exemption of the *"ab acatholicis nati"* in any form of real commentary, but the almost unanimous

[5] Canon 1099, § 2.

[6] S. C. S. Off., litt. (*ad Ep. Harlemen.*) 6 apr. 1859—*Fontes*, n. 950.

[7] S. C. C., 1 febr. 1908, ad V—*Fontes*, n. 4344; *AAS*, III (1911), 163-164.

conclusion of those who wrote on this particular question was that the parentage had to be non-Catholic on both sides together with the condition the child be reared from infancy in heresy or schism. Among those who held the theory which required that both parents be non-Catholic, there were authors of outstanding recognition.[8]

There were at least two authors, however, who were not sure that there was need of postulating a non-Catholic parentage on both sides for establishing the exemption enacted in canon 1099, § 2. Leitner (1862-1929), calling to mind the decree of the Holy Office of 1911, proposed that even under the law of the Code the Holy Office might consider the marriage valid even if only one of the parents was a non-Catholic, provided that all the other conditions were present, and thought that even under the Code law such a marriage should be referred to the Holy See for adjudication regarding its status.[9]

Jone accepted Leitner's view, and though in the face of so much worthy opposition he proceeded cautiously and proposed that the question would need special judgment by the Holy See, there is no doubt that he was personally certain that the phrase *"ab acatholicis nati"* in canon 1099, § 2, postulated no more than that one of the parents of the child who was baptized in the Catholic Church but reared from infancy outside of the Church be a non-Catholic.[10]

Against those who argued from the plural form of the wording

[8] Knecht, *Handbuch des katholischen Eherechts* (Freiburg: Herder, 1928), p. 652; Wernz-Vidal, *Ius Canonicum* (7 vols. in 8, Romae: apud Aedes Univ. Greg., 1923-1938), vol. V *Ius Matrimonial* (2 ed. 1928), n. 552; Vlaming, *Praelectiones Iuris Matrimonii* (3. ed., 2 vols., Bussum: Brand, 1919-1921), II, n. 599; Cappello, *Tractatus Canonico-Moralis de Sacramentis* (3 vols., Vol. III, Taurini: Marietti, 1923), III, n. 701, not. 3; Augustine, *A Commentary on the New Code of Canon Law* (8 vols., Vol. V, St. Louis: Herder, 1919), V, 302; Vermeersch-Creusen, *Epitome Iuris Canonici* (2. ed., 3 vols., Mechliniae: Dessain, 1925), II, 407, n. 2 (hereafter referred to as *Epitome*); DeSmet, *Tractatus Theologico-Canonicus de Sponsalibus et Matrimonio* (4. ed., Brugis: Beyaert, 1927), n. 143; Aertnys-Damen, *Theologia Moralis* (11. ed., 2 vols., Taurini-Romae: Marietti, 1928), II, n. 845.

[9] *Lehrbuch des katholischen Eherechts* (3. ed., Paderborn: Schöningh, 1920), p. 210.

[10] Jone, "Die Verpflichtung der Form bei der Eheschliessung"—*Theologish-praktisch Quartalschrift* (Linz, 1832—), LXXX (1927), 556-559.

of canon 1099, § 2, as postulating two non-Catholic parents (*ab acatholicis*), Jone pointed out that this specific form of wording by no means demanded such an interpretation, since the canon also used the plural form *"nati"* and not *"natus."* Thus philologically it was not postulated that there be two non-Catholics according to the words of the canon, for one could readily imagine two children born of different mixed marriages and rightfully regard both of the children as born (*nati*) of non-Catholics (*ab acatholicis*). Moreover, Jone continued, canon 751, in speaking of the baptism of the children of heretics expressly used the words *"circa baptismum infantium duorum haereticorum."* Hence, since one could safely conclude that in canon 1099, § 2, an equally unequivocal terminology is wanting, it is not necessary to postulate two non-Catholics, and therefore it suffices to postulate one.[11]

Again, Jone pointed out, in canon 1032, which treats of the permission requisite outside of the case of necessity for lawful assistance at the marriage of *"vagi,"* the lawgiver uses the word "marriage" in the singular form (*matrimonio*) and the word *"vagi"* in the plural form (*vagorum*), yet all authors who treated the point admitted that the norm of the canon was to be observed even though only one of the parties of the marriage was a *vagus*. Why could one not, therefore, apply the same reasoning to canon 1099, § 2, and maintain that one non-Catholic parent sufficed to warrant the exemption from the Code legislation for the *"ab acatholicis nati"*? [12]

[11] Canon 751: "Circa baptismum infantium duorum haereticorum aut schismaticorum, aut duorum catholicorum qui in apostasiam vel haeresim vel schisma prolapsi sunt, generatim serventur normae in superiore canone constitutae."

[12] Canon 987, which includes the children of non-Catholics among those who are impeded from the reception of Orders, uses the terms: *"Filii acatholicorum."* In 1919, the Pontifical Commission for the Interpretation of the Code, in answer to a doubt, declared that it sufficed that only one of the parents be a non-Catholic, and that this was true even when the mixed marriage was contracted with a dispensation, and the *cautiones* had been given.—*AAS*, II (1919), 478. Vermeersch-Creusen, however, denied that this interpretation of the term *"acatholicorum"* could be applied by private authority alone in support of the sufficiency of one non-Catholic parent for constituting a case in which the child could be regarded as born of non-Catholic parentage in the language of canon 1099, § 2.—*Epitome,* II, 407, n. 2.

Weighing all these intrinsic arguments, Jone concluded that their value seemed enough to create a real *dubium iuris,* and that therefore the marriage of a person baptized in the Catholic Church but reared outside of the Church from infancy must be considered valid when contracted without the observance of the canonical form even if only one of his parents was a non-Catholic. The validity of such a marriage had to be acknowledged at least in view of the doubt of law, if not also in consequence of the real and true meaning of the law. Jone himself, reinforcing his intrinsic arguments with the principle that odious things are to be restricted, actually thought the wording of the law to be sufficiently plain to protect such a marriage against the odium of invalidity.

In a later article, Jone referred to a case solved by the Holy Office, in which the marriage contracted by a non-Catholic girl with a man born of a Catholic mother and a non-Catholic father, but reared from infancy outside of the Church, was upheld as valid, even though the marriage was entered upon before a civil minister. The case was decided before the publication of a response of the Pontifical Commission for the Interpretation of the Code which solved the dispute, but the reply itself of the Pontifical Commission antedated the solution of the Holy Office.[13]

The reply of the Pontifical Commission given on July 20, 1929, settled the question of the meaning of the phrase *"ab acatholicis nati"* in relation to mixed marriages. It opposed the almost unanimous opinion of authors, and definitely established what might be called the tendency of Leitner and the conviction of Jone. It indicated that the persons *"ab acatholicis nati"* as mentioned in canon 1099, § 2, include also persons born of parents of whom only one is a non-Catholic, even when the *cautiones* have been given in accordance with canon 1061 and canon 1071.[14]

[13] Jone, "Die Verpflichtung der Form bei der Eheschliessung"—*Theologisch-praktische Quartalschrift,* LXXXII (1929), 780-783.

[14] Pont. Comm. Intr., 20 iul. 1929: D.—An ab acatholicis nati, de quibus in canon 1099, § 2, dicendi sint etiam nati ab alterutro parente acatholico, cautionibus quoque praestitis ad normam canonum 1061 et 1071. R. Affirmative.—*AAS,* XXI (1929), 573.

Article 3. Canon 1099, § 2, and Apostates

The response of July 20, 1929, was startling to the canonical world. Immediately authors turned their attention to the question whether the response of the Pontifical Commission for the Interpretation of the Code was declarative or extensive. With the common opinion postulating the presence of two non-Catholics in fulfillment of the condition of non-Catholic parentage, some thought that the answer of the Pontifical Commission was extensive rather than declarative, and that therefore it needed promulgation. Correspondingly they felt that the interpretation did not affect the marriages previously contracted without the observance of the canonical form by people born of parents of whom only one was a non-Catholic. This point will be considered more extensively in the following article, but it is mentioned here to establish the opinion that canonical writers on this question, few as they were, were more absorbed with the discussion of the nature of the response of 1929 with regard to its retroactivity in the case of mixed marriages than with any further discussion as to any other classes that might be included under the term. It may have been, too, that they were convinced of, and considered as needing no comment, the fact that apostates were included under the term *"ab acatholicis,"* and therefore had never discussed the point even in their earliest commentaries on the Code of Canon Law. The Pontifical Commission in a response given on February 11, 1930, included apostates under the term *"ab acatholicis"* of canon 1099, § 2.[15]

Article 4. The Nature of the First Response

When the response of the Pontifical Commission of 1929 became known to the world, there followed some speculation as to its nature. Was it declarative or extensive? The question was not without its importance both theoretically and practically. If the response was a declaration, then it stated what was clear in the law, was retroactive in force and did not need promulgation. If, however, the response

[15] Pont. Comm. Intr., 17 febr. 1930: D.—An sub verbis "ab acatholicis nati" de quibus in canone 1099, § 2, comprehendantur etiam nati ab apostatis. R.—Affirmative—*AAS,* XXII (1930), 195.

was extensive, that is, if it included matter or subjects not in the law from the beginning, then it had practically all the effects of a new law, was not retroactive and accordingly needed promulgation.[16]

For practical life this was not without significance. If the interpretation was extensive, then the marriages entered upon without the observance of the canonical form by people baptized as Catholics, if born of parents of whom only one was a non-Catholic, but reared from infancy in heresy, schism, or without any religion, were invalid in the event that these marriages had taken place before the response became effective in accordance with the rule regarding promulgation as enacted in canon 9. The solution of the point, then, was not of little importance.

There was an opinion that favored the theory of extensive interpretation. It seemed to those who were of this opinion, that weighing all things and taking into account the almost unanimous teaching of authors before the Pontifical Commission's first response, they could rightfully regard the response as clearly extensive,[17] and that therefore it needed promulgation. Relying on the rule of canon 9 with reference to the norms of promulgation, and considering moreover that the response made its appearance in the *"Acta Apostolicae Sedis"* under date of September 2, 1929, they concluded that the response obtained the force of law only three months later, on December 2, 1929.

However, the theory which favored the extensive character of the interpretation did not in consequence consider invalid all the previous marriages contracted without the observance of the canonical form by people baptized as Catholics, but who had been born of parents of whom only one was a non-Catholic and who later were lost to active Catholic membership in their religion even from infancy. It held rather that in spite of the preponderant external authority which postulated the presence of two non-Catholic parents as a con-

[16] Canon 17, § 2: "Interpretatio authentica per modum legis exhibita, eandem vim habet ac lex ipsa, et si verba legis certa declaret tantum, promulgatione non eget et valet retrorsum; si legem coarctet vel extendat aut dubium explicet, non retrotrahitur et debet promulgari."

[17] Cf. Schaaf, "An Exemption from the Canonical Form of Marriage"—*The Ecclesiastical Review,* LXXXIII (1930), 484-496.

dition for their progeny's exemption from the law of canon 1099, § 2, there was nevertheless sufficient intrinsic argument on the side of the minority opinion to establish a real doubt of law, and that therefore the marriages of such persons were, because of this doubt of law, to be considered valid.[18]

The supporters of the extensive character of the interpretation held substantially that the marriages of people baptized as Catholics, when born of parents of whom only one was a non-Catholic, that is, of parents who were united in a mixed marriage, and when reared from infancy outside the Church, even though the canonical form had not been observed in the celebration of these marriages, were:

1. Valid, if contracted after December 2, 1929, the time when the extensive interpretation, according to their opinion, obtained binding force.

2. Valid, even if contracted between Pentecost, 1918, when the present Code came into effect, and December 2, 1929, when, as they opined, the extensive interpretation obtained its binding force. This they based upon their conviction that the phrase "*ab acatholicis nati*" involved a doubt of law, and that consequently the law of canon 1099, § 2, which referred to the "*ab acatholicis nati*" did not achieve any binding force.

Practically, therefore, they safeguarded all marriages of this nature, provided that the parties had married no one who was himself bound to observe the canonical form.[19]

The supporters of the declarative character of the interpretation reasoned differently. They saw in the response of the Code Commission a mere declaration of an already palpably certain meaning of the terms of the canon. Maroto, for example, adding to the arguments already proposed by Jone, emphasized the importance of the response of the Pontifical Commission on the meaning of the words "*filii acatholicorum*" as contained in canon 987, 1°, which determined that one non-Catholic parent sufficed to make operative the require-

[18] Schaaf, *loc. cit.*

[19] Vermeersch-Creusen, *Epitome,* II, 407, n. 2; Creusen, *Nouvelle Revue Theologique* (Paris, 1869—), LVII (1930), 66; Maroto, "De vi verborum can. 1099, § 2: 'ab acatholicis nati'"—*Apollinaris* (Romae, 1928—), III (1930), 601-616.

ments of the canon, and considered it a certain and safe norm to follow also in relation to the meaning of the phrase *"ab acatholicis nati"* as contained in canon 1099, § 2.[20]

In the light of all the intrinsic reasons, and in view also of the fact that the purpose of the law, namely a gracious consideration for those who had fallen from the faith without any fault of their own, was as well served in the case of one non-Catholic parent as in the case of two, Maroto thought that the interpretation of the Pontifical Commission of 1929, when it stated that a mixed marriage sufficed to establish an exemption from the Catholic form of marriage according to the norms of canon 1099, § 2, was not extensive, but rather declarative. According to this theory, then, the response needed no promulgation and was retroactive in force.[21]

Maroto admitted, however, that most of the canonists who treated the subject thought the response extensive in character, though many did not treat the subject at all. He admitted as a natural consequence that there was in this question of the nature of the response a doubt of law, and came to the following practical conclusions.

1. For those who like himself considered the response of 1929 declarative, no question could be raised regarding the presumable validity of the marriages contracted without the Catholic form on the part of those who were born of mixed marriages, were baptized in the Catholic Church and then were reared from infancy outside of the Church, as long as they married non-Catholics. These marriages were to be considered valid, since a declarative interpretation needs no promulgation and has retroactive force.

2. For those who held that the interpretation was extensive in its character, such marriages were in and of themselves invalid before the promulgation of the response became binding law, but he considered the whole question to involve a doubt of law, and concluded in accordance with the legal principle of canon 15 that because of the doubt of law the marriages should be considered valid. In any event, as long as the doubt existed, the marriages which were contracted before the issuance of the response could not be safely

[20] Maroto, *loc. cit.*

[21] Canon 17, § 2.

declared null, since in doubt the presumable validity of the marriage enjoyed the favor of the law.[22]

It is clear from a consideration of the two opinions that, though they differed theoretically and entailed even grave theoretical consequences, both sides endeavored to safeguard the validity of the marriages in all practical cases. The theory that the interpretation was simply declarative bore of course no grave practical consequences, inasmuch as for the meaning of the terms of the declaration there was implied a retroactive force; but in the theory that the interpretation was of an extensive character there was no room for retroactivity in the newly interpreted meaning of the law. Consequently, before the ruling of the Pontifical Commission could take effect attendant upon the necessary lapse of time after the legitimate promulgation, the marriages contracted in the interim without the observance of the canonical form on the part of people who as the offspring of a mixed marriage had indeed received a Catholic baptism, but had not been reared in the faith, had in principle to be considered invalid. However, the exponents of both theories rallied around the doubt of law that existed in the case, and with reference simply to the disputed requirement of a canonical form upheld the validity of all the marriages contracted by people born of a mixed marriage, provided that all the other postulated conditions as mentioned in canon 1099, § 2, were duly fulfilled and actually present.

There was such disagreement on the point, and the true nature of the response could have such practical consequences, that an official interpretation of the nature of the response seemed necessary. The problem centered around the validity of the marriages contracted before the response of 1929 and entered upon outside the Church by persons born of mixed marriages and reared from infancy in heresy, when earlier they had been baptized as Catholics; if the response implied an extensive interpretation such marriages were in principle invalid.[23]

In a marriage case submitted to it by the Archdiocesan Curia of

[22] Canon 1014: "Matrimonium gaudet favore iuris: quare in dubio standum est pro valore matrimonii donec contrarium probetur, salvo praescripto can. 1127."

[23] *Supra*, p. 18.

St. Louis, the Holy Office decided that the marriage of a girl, Sophia, who was born of a Catholic mother and a non-Catholic father, and who had been baptized in the Catholic Church but was reared from infancy out of the Church, was valid, even though she had married a Lutheran man before the justice of the peace in the year 1922.[24] This solution of the Holy Office was given on June 9, 1931. According to this solution the interpretation of 1929 had to be regarded as being retrocative in its juridical effects and efficacy. However, in the same year the Holy Office reserved to itself the right to decide on the validity of such marriages which had been contracted before the publication of the decision of the Pontifical Commission, but notice of the making of this reservation was never made public.[25]

This reservation seemed to imply that the Holy Office thought the answer of the Pontifical Commission to be explanatory rather than declarative.[26] On the other hand, it may also have been that the Holy Office recognized the validity of the marriage because of the doubt of law that was commonly thought to exist, and which had been generally admitted by canonical writers.[27] In any event, only a little more than a month after this solution of the Holy Office, the Pontifical Commission, in answer to a question concerning the nature of the response of July 20, 1929, in which the progeny of mixed marriages, even when these were entered upon with the cautiones, was included under the terms *"ab acatholicis nati"* of canon 1099, § 2, said that this response was declarative.[28]

The issue was settled. The response of the Pontifical Commission of 1929 was, therefore, retroactive in force and needed no promulgation. Marriages contracted before December 2, 1929 by

[24] S. C. S. Off., 9 ian. 1931—*Periodica de Re Canonica et Morali utili praesertim Religiosis et Missionariis* (Brugis, 1905-1927); *Periodica de Re Morali, Canonica, Liturgica* (Brugis, 1928-1936; Romae, 1937—), XXI (1932), 14 (hereafter referred to as *Periodica*). Bouscaren, *The Canon Law Digest* (2 vols., Milwaukee: Bruce Publishing Co., 1934-1943), I, 544.

[25] *Periodica,* XXI (1932), 46.

[26] *Periodica,* XXI (1932), 14 and 26.

[27] Cf. *supra,* p. 18.

[28] Pont. Comm. Intr., 20 iul. 1931: D.—Utrum interpretatio diei 20 iulii 1929 ad canonem 1099, § 2, sit declarativa an extensiva. R.—Affirmative ad primam partem, negative ad secundam.—*AAS,* XXIII (1931), 388.

children born of mixed marriages, even when for the latter the *cautiones* had been given, were thus upheld as valid despite the non-observance of the canonical form, provided that the other postulated conditions of canon 1099, § 2, were verified. Such marriages needed no doubt of law to support their claim to validity. Such had been the law from the beginning. This, then, was the significance of the declarative nature of the response of 1929, as determined by the Pontifical Commission in its answer of July 20, 1931.[29]

Article 5. Apostates Included under the Phrase *"Ab Acatholicis"*

A response of the Code Commission given in 1930 included apostates under the phrase *"ab acatholicis."*[30] Before this response there was an opinion that had excluded them.[31] This opinion was based on the idea that the apostate parents themselves were bound to observe the form even though they had fallen from the faith; but, though this was true and though the apostates themselves were considered Catholics as far as the obligation to observe the form of marriage was concerned after they had fallen from the faith nevertheless they were not Catholics in other respects. Canon 1099, § 2, did not create an exemption for the apostates themselves, but it did exempt their children, provided that the other conditions of the canon were fulfilled. Briefly, this opinion, in considering that apostates from the faith were bound to the Catholic form of marriage, thought of them as Catholics in relation to the Church's marriage laws, and therefore concluded that those who were born of them were to be considered as born of Catholics. But canon 1099 nowhere calls such apostates Catholics; it merely obliges them to the Catholic form of marriage. They are themselves non-Catholic, and hence those who are born of them are to be considered as born of non-Catholics.[32]

Moreover, it is to be recalled that canon 1325, after defining in

[29] Cf. *Jus Pontificium* (Romae, 1921), XI (1931), 256; canon 17, § 2.

[30] Pont. Comm. Intr., 17 febr. 1930—*AAS,* XXII (1930), 195.

[31] De Smet, *Tractatus Theologico-Canonicus de Sponsalibus et Matrimonio,* n. 140.

[32] Maroto, "De vi verborum can. 1099, § 2: 'ab acatholicis nati' "—*Apollinaris,* III (1930), 601-616.

§ 2 an apostate as one who has totally fallen from the Christian faith, does not exclude them from but rather seems to include them under the general term *"acatholici,"* as employed in the same canon in § 3. Again, when one considers that the condition of persons born of apostates is even worse than that of persons born of heretics or of schismatics, and inasmuch as the purpose of the exemption of canon 1099, § 2, is to safeguard the validity of the marriages of children born of such parents, which children through no fault of their own were reared outside the Church and then married outside of the Church, one may readily regard such persons as sharing in the exemption of the *"ab acatholicis nati."* [33] The response of the Pontifical Commission, as treated above, ended all discussion and definitely includes apostates under the phrase *"ab acatholicis."* The preceding discussion is now only history.

An apostate is defined in the Code as one who totally lapses from the Christian Faith.[34] But in the application of this term to the wording of canon 1099, § 2, in view of the response of the Pontifical Commission which included apostates under the phrase *"ab acatholicis,"* it is commonly taught that the term "apostate," besides being taken in the stricter sense of one who has completely rejected the Christian faith, includes also everyone who has lapsed from the Catholic faith, even though he may never have become an infidel, everyone who has left the Catholic Church to join some schismatical or heretical sect in which case he seems to fall likewise under the more specific classification of a heretic, or of a schismatic, and also everyone who in any way has defected from the Catholic faith which he once professed. This teaching emphasizes the fact that not the apostates themselves, but their children in whom are verified the other postulated conditions of canon 1099, § 2, are exempt from the canonical form of marriage. The reasons supporting the acceptance of the word "apostate" in the wider sense as included under canon 1099, § 2, are mainly the tenor of the canon, which is the protection of the blameless children, and the decision of the Holy See, which

[33] *Jus Pontificium,* X (1930), 143-144.
[34] Canon 1325, § 2.

allowed the wider interpretation of the word "apostate" for other canons.[85]

There has been no similar decision relative to the present canon under consideration, but the wider comprehensiveness of the term in relation also to canon 1099 § 2 is supported by the common teaching.[86] The teaching, however, postulates a real defection from the faith, and not a mere status or condition of indifference or of negligence. Consequently carelessness in the practice of one's religion, neglect of one's Easter duty, negligence about one's attendance at Sunday Mass, or even affiliation with Freemasonry or with some other forbidden society, do not of themselves constitute apostasy.[87] However, if a Catholic publicly becomes an atheist in his sectarian profession,[88] or a materialist, or a freethinker, or formally embraces heresy or schism, or joins a pagan cult or some society which actually professes heresy or schism, he is without doubt to be considered an apostate.[89] A child born of erstwhile Catholic parents who have thus

[85] The Holy Office employed the wider meaning of "apostate" in relation to the denial of the right of impugning the validity of a marriage in procedural law—*Periodica,* XXVI (1937), 400; *AAS,* XXXII (1940), 52.

[86] Maroto, *loc. cit.*; Vermeersch-Creusen, "Adnotationes"—*Periodica,* XIX (1930), 268-269; *Jus Pontificium,* X (1930), 143-144; Cappello, "Quinam censeantur 'ab acatholicis nati' ad normam can. 1099, § 2, ideoque a canonica forma celebrationis matrimonii immunes"—*Periodica,* XX (1931), 77; Schaaf, "An Exemption from the Canonical Form of Marriage"—*The Ecclesiastical Review,* LXXXIII (1930), 488-496; Bareille, *Code du Droit Canonique* (2. éd., Paris: Cordeilhac-Soubiron, 1925), n. 296; Mahoney, "'Ab Acatholicis Nati' (can. 1099, § 2)"—*The Clergy Review* (London, 1931—), XVI (1939), 511-520.

[87] Doheny, *Canonical Procedure in Matrimonial Cases* (Milwaukee: Bruce Publishing Co., 1938), p. 667; Cappello, *loc. cit.*—*Periodica,* XX (1931), 80.

[88] The Pontifical Commission for the Interpretation of the Code was asked: "An ad normam Codicis Iuris Canonici qui sectae atheisticae adscripti sunt vel fuerunt, habendi sint quoad omnes iuris effectus, etiam in ordine ad sacram ordinationem et matrimonium, ad instar eorum qui sectae acatholicae adhaerent vel adhaeserunt?" The Commission answered: "Affirmative."—*AAS,* XXVI (1934), 494.

[89] Carberry, *The Juridical Form of Marriage,* The Catholic University of America Canon Law Studies, n. 84 (Washington, D. C.: The Catholic University of America, 1934), p. 132; Cappello, "Quinam censeantur 'ab acatholicis nati' ad normam canon 1099, § 2, ideoque a canonica forma celebrationis Matri-

defected from the Catholic Church can be said to be *"natus ab apostatis,"* provided that the apostasy took place before the child's birth.[40] The condition of the canon is fulfilled if even only one of the parents is an apostate. This is the unanimous opinion of canonists, and it is certain from an analogy with the first decision of the Pontifical Commission, which declared that one non-Catholic parent sufficed to fulfill the condition of the law exempting the child from the form of marriage.[41]

monii Immunes"—*Periodica de re Canonica et Morali Utili Praesertim Religiosis et Missionariis* (Bruges, 1905—), XV (1931), p. 77.

[40] Maroto, *loc. cit.*—*Apollinaris,* III (1930), 612.

[41] Cf. *supra,* p. 17; Cappello, *loc. cit.*—*Periodica,* XX (1931), 77; Ayrinhac-Lydon, *Marriage Legislation in the New Code of Canon Law* (2. revised ed. by P. J. Lydon, New York: Benziger Brothers, 1938), p. 256.

SUMMARY

As a summary of the preceding discussion the following are to be considered born of non-Catholics as understood in canon 1099, § 2:

1. A child born of two heretics or schismatics whether or not they enrolled in a heretical or a schismatical sect.

2. A child born of one Catholic parent and one parent that is a heretic or schismatic whether or not the latter be enrolled in a heretical or a schismatical sect even though the marriage was contracted with the previous furnishing of the *cautiones* according to canon 1061.

3. A child born of parents both of whom are non-baptized.

4. A child born of one non-Catholic parent who is baptized and of one parent who is unbaptized.

5. A child born of one Catholic parent and of one parent who is unbaptized, even though the marriage was contracted with the previous furnishing of *cautiones* according to canon 1071.

6. A child born of two apostate parents in the sense of canon 1325, § 2, i. e., born of two parents who have totally rejected the Christian faith.

7. A child born of one Christian parent who is a non-Catholic and of one parent who is an apostate in the sense of canon 1325, § 2.

8. A child born of one Catholic parent and of one parent who is an apostate in the sense of canon 1325, § 2.

9. A child born of two apostates, in the broad sense of the term, i.e., born of two parents who have publicly given up, not the Christian faith, but the Catholic Faith. Mere negligence on the part of the parents towards Catholicism, however, does not of itself indicate apostasy.

10. A child born of one Catholic parent and of one parent who is an apostate in the broad sense of the term.

11. A child born of parents who are professedly atheists, materialists, freethinkers, or who have formally embraced heresy or schism, or who have joined a pagan cult or some society which actually professes heresy or schism.

It suffices that only one of the parents falls under any of these groups and that his condition of being a non-Catholic obtains at the time of the birth of the child in question.[42]

ARTICLE 6. PERSONS BORN OF TWO CATHOLIC PARENTS IN RELATION TO THE EXEMPTION OF CANON 1099, § 2.

The three decisions of the Pontifical Commission for the Interpretation of the Code ended the discussion on the meaning of the phrase *"ab acatholicis nati" of canon* 1099, § 2. That question is now settled. A child born of a mixed marriage, or of parents who have apostatized, or of whom only one parent has apostatized before his birth, is not bound to the Catholic form of marriage if reared outside the Catholic Church, even though the child was baptized in the Catholic Church. The strict interpretation to which the law was subjected [43] as an exception to the general rule had led canonical writers to require that both parents be non-Catholic. Even after the decision which stated that those who were born of mixed marriages were included under the phrase *"ab acatholicis nati,"* many thought that this was an extension of the law and accordingly required a promulgation, and thus there was need of another decision for settling this question and for vouching that the first decision was simply declarative.[44]

But now there arose a new question. The decision taught substantially that the child had to be born of at least one non-Catholic parent in order to fall within the classification of *"ab acatholicis nati"* of canon 1099, § 2. Less than that could not suffice. The wording of the law could not be satisfied with anything less. The law clearly refers to those who, when born of non-Catholics, suffer the misfortune of being reared outside the Catholic Church after their Catholic baptism in infancy; but some few canonical writers endeavored to

[42] In the mind of the Church on marriage, heretics and schismatics of Oriental rites are included under the term non-Catholics, so that a person who is born of heretical or schismatical parents, or of parents of whom only one is a heretic or a schismatic, can be said to be born *"ab acatholicis."* Cf. S. C. C., *Romana et Aliarum,* 28 mart. 1908, ad II—*Fontes,* n. 4349.

[43] Cf. *supra,* p. 17.

[44] Cf. *supra,* p. 24.

extend the law to include also those, who, when born of two Catholic parents, suffer the same misfortune of being reared from infancy outside of the Church in spite of their Catholic baptism.

Thus Triebs maintained that a child born of Catholic parents, when baptized in the Catholic Church, but reared in heresy, schism, infidelity, or without any religion, was not bound by the form of marriage, inasmuch as he never willingly and knowingly belonged to the Catholic Church.[45] Sipos also thought that children born of Catholic parents are exempt from the form of marriage, even though they were baptized in the Catholic Church, if in consequence of the subsequent apostasy of the parents they were reared from infancy outside of the Catholic Church; but he hesitated to say that they are exempt if they were reared outside of the Catholic Church by others in whose care they had fallen as a result of the death of the parents.[46]

If one wishes to argue primarily from the purpose of the law, as did Sipos, it is difficult to see on what grounds he made the distinction, for the purpose of the law call for a like adjustment in both cases, since in both the child is reared from infancy outside of the Church through no fault of its own; but Sipos simply invoked the distinction without indicating any reasons for doing so.

That children born of Catholics but reared outside the Church are exempt from the form is also the opinion of an undisclosed writer in the *Ecclesiastical Review,* who believed that it did not matter whether the parents apostatized before or after the birth of the child, provided that the child was reared outside the Church, since in either case the condition of the child was the same. He suggested therefore that the ordinary should refer such a case to the Holy See.[47]

Oesterle and Leitner admitted that in such a case as this, namely when the Catholic parents of children who have been baptized in the Catholic Church apostatized before the children reach the age of reason, with the result that the children themselves are reared outside

[45] *Praktisches Handbuch des geltenden kanonischen Eherechts in Vergleichung mit dem deutschen staatlichen Eherecht* (Teil I-IV in einem Band, Gesamtausgabe, Breslau: Ostdeutsche Verlagsanstalt, 1933), p. 610 (hereafter referred to as *Handbuch des kanonischen Eherechts*).

[46] *Enchiridion Iuris Canonici* (3. ed., Pécs: Haladás R.T., 1936), p. 602.

[47] *The Ecclesiastical Review,* LXXXIX (1933), 69-76.

the Church, the children cannot literally be said to be born *"ab acatholicis"* since their parents were Catholics at the time of their birth, and hence these children do not strictly come under the exemption of canon 1099, § 2; but these two authors nevertheless contended that the spirit of the law is the same, and thus calls for its extension to the case of those who are born of Catholics and baptized in the Catholic Church, but reared outside the Church through no fault of their own. Both Oesterle and Leitner conceded, however, that their conclusions militated against the literal meaning of the law, and thus were far from certain.[48]

Schaaf shares in the hesitancy of Oesterle and Leitner, and does not think that the opinion enjoys any probability. He concludes accordingly that to regard as exempt from the form those who are born of Catholics, even though all the other conditions of canon 1099, § 2, be fulfilled, would require an extensive interpretation of the law on the part of the Holy See.[49]

When one considers the wording of the Code in the exemption which is extended to those who are baptized outside of the Church, it appears evident that the opinion as held by Triebs and Sipos is untenable. The Code expressly states that only those who are born of non-Catholics are exempt from the form provided that the other conditions of canon 1099, § 2, are fulfilled. This is admitted even by those who propose the opinion that would extend the exemption also to those who are born of Catholic parents. Moreover, the canon enacts an exception to the general law that all those who are baptized in the Catholic Church are bound to the Catholic form of marriage.[50] It is even expressly referred to as an exception in canon 1094, which states that only those marriages are valid which are contracted before the pastor or ordinary of the place or before a priest delegated by either and before two witnesses according to the

[48] Oesterle, "Form der Eheschliessung für die *'nati ab acatholicis,'* canon 1099, § 2"—*Theologisch-praktische Quartalschrift,* LXXXV (1932), 352-361; Leitner, *Handbuch des katholischen Kirchenrechts* (5 vols., Regensburg: Kösel-Pustet, 1921-1927, Vol. IV, 2. ed., 1924), IV, 243.

[49] "Are children born of Catholics exempt from canonical form of marriage?"—*The Ecclesiastical Review,* XCIV (1936), 632-633.

[50] Canon 1099, § 1.

canons which follow *"et salvis exceptionibus de quibus in can.* 1098, 1099." As an exception to the general law, then, canon 1099, § 2, must be interpreted strictly.[51]

The canon speaks of persons *"ab acatholicis nati."* Such clarity of wording in a law which is subject to strict interpretation cannot be extended or expanded to include also those who are born of Catholic parents. A law must be understood according to the proper signification of the words in the law. To extend the present law to include those who are born of Catholic parents is to extend it beyond its obvious intent.[52]

The phrase "non-Catholic parents" can never be made to include Catholic parents. Before the latter could be dealt with on a basis of parity with non-Catholic parents, a fundamental change would have to be effected in the law. This is also the opinion of Cappello who states that those who are born of Catholic parents and are baptized in the Catholic Church, but who were reared from infancy outside of the Catholic Church, are nevertheless bound to observe the canonical form of marriage.[53] It is, in fact, the opinion of the overwhelming majority of canonical writers. Thus Farrugia, Vlaming (+1935), Chelodi (+1922), Cerato, Payen, Raus (+1943), Vromant, Prümmer (+1931), Vermeersch (+1936)-Creusen, Aertnys (+1915)-Damen all taught that those who are born of Catholic parents do not enjoy the exemption from the form, even though the other conditions of canon 1099, § 2, are fulfilled.[54] Many other writers do not treat the point at all.

[51] Canon 19.

[52] Canon 18; Maroto, "De vi verborum can. 1099, § 2: 'ab acatholicis nati' " —*Apollinaris,* III (1930), 608.

[53] Cappello, *Tractatus Canonico—Moralis De Sacramentis* (Vol. III, 4. ed., Romae: apud Aedes Univ. Gregorianae, 1939), III, nn. 702, 794 (hereafter referred to as *De Matrimonio*).

[54] Farrugia, *De Matrimonio et Causis Matrimonialibus—Tractatus Canonico-moralis iuxta Codicem Iuris Canonici* (Taurini-Romae: Marietti, 1924), n. 238; Vlaming, *Praelectiones Iuris Matrimonii,* n. 598; Chelodi, *Ius Matrimoniale* (4. ed., a V. Dalpiaz, Tridenti: Libreria Moderna Editrice A. Ardesi, 1937), n. 126; Cerato, *Matrimonium a Codice Iuris Canonici Integre Desumptum* (4. ed., Patavii: Typis Seminarii, 1929), p. 166, n. 96; Payen, *De Matrimonio,* II, n. 1840; Raus, *Institutiones Canonicae* (2. ed., Londini-Parisiis: Emmanuel Vitte, 1931), p. 484, n. 313; Vromant, *Ius Missionorum,* Vol. V, *De Matrimonio*

Furthermore, the exclusion of those born of Catholic parents from the exemption of the class of persons born of non-Catholic parents (*"ab acatholicis nati"*) is emphasized by the brief history of the law. When the exemption from the form for baptized Catholics was first decreed for Holland, it was extended to the following classes of people:

1. Those baptized in the Catholic Church, but who were reared in heresy or who professed heresy from earliest childhood (*a pueritia nondum septennali*).

2. Those baptized in the Catholic Church, but educated by heretics, even though they received little education in heresy and though they had not been very notably active in heresy or heretical sects.

3. Those baptized in the Catholic Church who when yet in childhood had fallen under the influence of heretics and had joined a heretical sect.

4. Apostates from the Catholic Church who had gone over to heretical sects.

5. Those born of heretics and baptized by heretics, even though they had never professed loyalty to any heretical sect or to any religion.[55]

With the exception of the last group, nothing was said in the decree of 1859 about the Catholic or non-Catholic affiliation of the parents of these children, and consequently this point did not enter the discussion at all. Thus in the first group as listed by the Holy Office in 1859, nothing was said about the Catholic or non-Catholic affiliation of the parents of the children. All that was required to induce the exemption from the form was that the child, though baptized in the Catholic Church, be reared in heresy or profess heresy

(Louvain: Museum Lessianum, 1931), 176, n. 215 (hereafter referred to as *De Matrimonio*); Aertnys-Damen, *Theologia Moralis* (13. ed., 2 vols., Taurini-Romae: Marietti, 1939), n. 722; Prümmer, *Manuale Theologiae Moralis* (8. ed., 3 vols., Friburgi Brisgoviae: Herder & Co., 1935-1936), III, p. 548, n. 754; Vermeersch-Creusen, *Epitome Iuris Canonici* (3 vols., Mechliniae-Romae: H. Dessain, Vol. I, 6. ed., 1937; Vol. II, 5. ed., 1934; Vol. III, 5. ed., 1936), II, n. 407 (hereafter referred to as *Epitome*).

[55] S. C. S. Off., litt. (*ad Ep. Harlemen.*), 6 apr. 1859—*Fontes*, n. 950; cf. *supra*, p. 9.

from earliest childhood (*a pueritia nondum septennali*). The decree "*Ne temere*" abolished these exemptions,[56] and when the exemption appeared again, and now for the first time as general in the Code, the law was expressed in different terms. The Code clearly restricts the favor of this exemption to those who are born of non-Catholic parents. It seems even to emphasize the point. In reading Canon 1099, § 2, one is reminded of this by means of the phrase "*firmo praescripto § 1, n.1*" where it is clearly stated that all who are baptized in the Church are held to the form. The only exception to this general rule is that the second paragraph of canon 1099 which requires for exemption the fact of being reared from infancy outside the Church and birth from non-Catholic parents.

Even when the Holy Office decreed in 1911 that recourse was required to be made to the Holy See *in singulis casibus* whenever there was a case to determine the validity of a marriage of a child born of non-Catholics if the child had been baptized a Catholic but reared from infancy outside of the Church and had contracted marriage with a non-Catholic without benefit of the legitimate form,[57] it was only a question of children born of non-Catholics. It had nothing to do with children born of Catholics; but even if it had included the latter, which it did not, that decree would have been abrogated since canon 1099, § 2 had now the force of law for the situation which the Holy Office then considered and reserved to itself for decision in each case.

It seems that those who would extend the phrase "*ab acatholicis nati*" of canon 1099, § 2, to mean "born of Catholics" ("*a catholicis nati*") want to insist more upon pre-Code law as found in the decree of the Holy Office sent to the Bishop of Haarlem, which exempted from the form of marriage those baptized in the Catholic Church but reared in heresy from earliest childhood (*a pueritia nondum septennali*), whether they were born of Catholic or of non-Catholic parents, than upon that legislation of the Code itself which requires birth from non-Catholic parents as a necessary condition.

No one can be found who denies that there may be reasons that

[56] Cf. S. C. C., 1 febr. 1908—*ASS*, XLI (1908), 108; Wernz, *Ius Decretalium*, IV, n. 188; *Fontes*, n. 4344.

[57] *AAS*, III (1911), 163-164; cf. *supra*, p. 14.

make it expedient that those baptized Catholics who are born of Catholic parents and who are reared from infancy outside of the Church should be likened to the "*ab acatholicis nati*" of as described in canon 1099, § 2. The purpose of the exemption as admitted by all is to free those children who were baptized in the Church but born of non-Catholic parents from the obligation to the Catholic form of marriage when through no fault of their own they have been reared outside of the Church from infancy. One can easily imagine, or perhaps recall from personal experience, cases in which children born of Catholic parents and baptized as Catholics were reared outside the Church with no more personal guilt or moral responsibility than that attached to those born of non-Catholic parents found in the same condition. It is this argument from the purpose of the law that those canonical writers insist upon in their wish to extend the exemption of the canon to those born of Catholic parentage when they share no guilt in their non-Catholic up-bringing.[58]

One might even be so bold as to say, should he so desire, that because of this reason the law is found wanting,[59] and that it would be desirable that those born of Catholic parents and in whom are fulfilled the other conditions of the law should be allowed to enjoy the exemption; but this would require the enactment of an extension by the law, since in its present state the law does not allow the exemption for any but for those who are born of non-Catholic parents. The lack of responsibility, or the freedom from guilt, may be present equally in those born of Catholic and non-Catholic parents; but these elements of responsibility constitute a moral issue. Here one deals in the juridic order where private interpretation or a desire to make a law what it is assumed it ought to be, even with the best of intentions, can effect nothing as to the meaning of that law.

Finally, though the cases of baptized Catholics born of Catholic parents but reared as non-Catholics in view of the death or subsequent apostasy of the parents can arise, they will not be as frequent, as in the circumstances of a non-Catholic parentage such as could arise for example in a mixed marriage. This is emphasized by the law itself when in recognizing the danger of such circumstances

[58] Sipos, *loc. cit.*; Triebs, *loc. cit.*; Leitner, *loc. cit.*

[59] Vermeersch-Creusen, *Epitome,* II, n. 407.

it requires special promises regarding the Catholic education of the children before the granting of a dispensation from the impediments of mixed religion and of disparity of cult.[60]

The legislator can be conceived as legislating for that which is more apt to happen rather than as attempting to safeguard the validity of every marriage that might be invalid because of the lack of observance of the Catholic form of marriage.[61] In any event, it is the will of the legislator clearly expressed in the law of canon 1099, § 2, that there is an exemption from the form of marriage for a certain class of persons baptized as Catholics but that one of the essential conditions of the exemption is birth from non-Catholic parents.[62]

It is difficult to see how any probability can be given to the opinion that would extend the exemption from the form to those born of Catholic parents, since no other exception is allowed.[63] That the parents must be non-Catholic, or at least one of them, at the time of the birth of the child to induce for the latter the exemption allowed in canon 1099, § 2, is clear from the canon itself.[64] Therefore, if both parents are Catholic at the time of the birth of the child, and if the child is baptized in the Catholic Church, the child is held to the Catholic form even though it was reared in heresy, schism or infidelity. A marriage contracted by such a person without the canonical form could safely be declared null *ex defectu formae.* The clear wording of the canon, the vast majority of the authors who support this opinion as certain, the history of the exemption itself, and the norms

[60] Canons 1061, § 1, n. 2; 1071.

[61] Dalpiaz, "An a catholicis nati et catholice baptizati, sed ab infantili aetate acatholice educati, praescripta matrimonii forma teneantur?"—*Apollinaris,* X (1937), 105-107.

[62] Maroto, "De vi verborum can. 1099, § 2: 'ab acatholicis nati' "—*Apollinaris,* III (1930), 601-616; *The Ecclesiastical Review,* CIII (1940), 284; Dalpiaz, "An a catholicis nati et catholice baptizati, sed ab infantili aetate acatholice educati, praescripta matrimonii forma teneantur"—*Apollinaris,* X (1937), 105-107.

[63] Wernz-Vidal, *Ius Canonicum,* V, n. 553; O'Donnell, "*Ne temere* and the New Code"—*The Irish Theological Quarterly* (Dublin-St. Louis, 1906—), XIV (1919), 155.

[64] Marx, *The Declaration of Nullity of Marriage Contracted Outside the Church* (The Catholic University of America Canon Law Studies, n. 182, Washington, D. C.: The Catholic University of America Press, 1943), p. 58.

for the interpretation of law all militate against the probability of any opinion that would extend the exemption to those who are born of Catholic parents. One cannot argue solely from the purpose of the law, and to include children born of Catholic parents under the phrase *"ab acatholicis nati"* is an attempt void of any intrinsic value, and clearly contrary to the law itself, at least in its present form.

There is a case, however, that presents new difficulties. What of a child born of non-Catholic parents and baptized in the Catholic Church when its parents were converted to the faith after the child's birth but then apostatized before the child reached the age of reason? The child seems to be exempt from all obligation to the form of marriage since both the letter and the purpose of canon 1099, § 2, are fulfilled.[65] It would at least certainly be unsound in practice to declare the marriage of such a person invalid for failure to observe the form.[66]

Article 7. Illegitimate Children and Foundlings

A question arises concerning the status of illegitimate children and their relation to canon 1099, § 2. The canon makes no distinction between children born of a valid marriage and those born out of wedlock. Nor was any such distinction made in the pre-Code legislation and jurisprudence for similar cases. The present law merely states that persons baptized in the Catholic Church but born of non-Catholics are free from the obligation of observing the canonical form of marriage whenever they marry non-Catholics, provided that the former (*"ab acatholicis nati"*) were reared from infancy in heresy, schism, infidelity or without any religion. The law makes no distinction between legitimate and illegitimate children. All that is required is that the child be born of non-Catholics. Once therefore it can be established that a child's parents were non-Catholics or at least one of them was a non-Catholic, at the time of the child's birth, the child can be said to be born of non-Catholics *("ab acatholicis")* in the sense of canon 1099, § 2, whether it is legitimate or illegitimate.

An objection may be brought to the effect that illegitimate chil-

[65] Hannan, "Validity of Marriage, Canons 1099 and 1070"—*The Ecclesiastical Review,* CIX (1943), 453-456.

[66] Hannan, *loc. cit.*

dren seem to follow the religion of the mother in such cases and that only if the mother is a non-Catholic can the child be considered to have been born of non-Catholics. This doctrine is implied by Augustine.[67] Thus the law determines that the place of origin (*locus originis*) of an illegitimate child is that place where the mother had her domicile or, in the event she had no domicile, her quasi-domicile at the time of the child's birth.[68]

An answer to the objection does not seem difficult. It is one thing to determine a child's place of origin, and another to determine the effects that flow from the religious affiliation of its parents. Canon 90 does not destroy the other juridical effects of the parentage of the father of an illegitimate child. It merely determines that the juridical status of the father's domicile or quasi-domicile will have no effect upon the determination of the place of origin of his illegitimate child, whereas it will determine that of a legitimate child.[69] The canon therefore expressly distinguishes between the norms that determine the place of origin for legitimate children and those that determine the place of origin for illegitimate children. Canon 1099, § 2, however, makes no such distinction. It is interested only in the Catholic or non-Catholic status of the parents. If the child's parents are non-Catholics, or if only one of them is a non-Catholic the condition of the canon is fulfilled. The child is "*natus ab acatholicis.*"

The law, moreover, wishes to exempt the "*ab acatholicis nati*" from the form of marriage when, in spite of their Catholic baptism, they are reared and educated from infancy outside the Catholic Church. The education of children will normally be determined by the parents themselves. But the parents of illegitimate children are in no way released from the obligations of parental care, and accordingly are obliged to provide for their welfare. The Code itself states that parents are bound by a very grave obligation to care for the religious and moral education of their children, as well as for their physical and civic needs.[70] It does not exempt the parents

[67] *A Commentary on Canon Law* (8 vols., Vol. V, 5. revised ed., St. Louis: Herder Book Co., 1935), V, 302.

[68] Canon 90, § 1.

[69] Canon 90, § 1.

[70] Canon 1113.

of illegitimate children from these parental obligations, nor does it limit such care to only one of the parents. The natural law itself obliges both parents of an illegitimate child to provide for its education and general welfare,[71] and the child will remain subject to the training provided by its parents.

Intrinsically, therefore, the position of the child relative to its education in infancy does not differ essentially whether it be legitimate or illegitimate. Nor is the case changed in the event that only one parent is a Catholic and that the illegitimate child is left solely to the care of the Catholic parent who rears it from infancy in heresy. The failure of the Catholic parent in such a case to provide for the Catholic training of the child will only be equivalent to that of the Catholic parent in a mixed marriage who fails to rear the child in Catholicism, even though the *cautiones* had been given before the marriage in accordance with canon 1061. In both cases the child is born of non-Catholics in the sense of canon 1099, § 2, and reared from infancy outside the Catholic Church through no fault of its own.[72] In either case both the letter and the purpose of the law are fulfilled in reference to the law's exemption and the child is released from the form of marriage even in the event that it had been baptized in the Catholic Church.

In cases involving foundlings and adopted children the same principles are sustained. Before the release from the obligation of observing the canonical form of marriage which canon 1099, § 2, allows can be claimed by a person baptized in the Catholic Church, it must be established that the party concerned was born of non-Catholic parents, or at least of one non-Catholic parent, and reared from infancy in heresy, schism, infidelity, or without any religion. If it cannot be established that the conditions of canon 1099, § 2, are fulfilled in the cases of persons under consideration, such persons cannot claim freedom from the obligation of observing the canonical form. In all cases of doubt the validity of the marriage would have to be upheld.[73]

[71] Prümmer, *Manuale Theologiae Moralis,* II, n. 586; Cappello, *De Matrimonio,* n. 742.

[72] Cf. *supra,* p. 18.

[73] Canon 1014.

CHAPTER V

INFANT BAPTISM AND CANON 1099, § 2

Article 1. Baptism in the Catholic Church

Everyone who is validly baptized is in reality baptized in the Catholic Church, since there is but one valid baptism. Thus canon 87 of the Code of Canon Law states that through baptism an individual is constituted a person in the Church of Christ with all the rights and offices (duties) of Christians unless, as regards his rights, there is some obstacle that impedes the exercise of these rights or he is subject to some censure.[1]

As regards the obligation to observe the Catholic form of marriage, however, there is a distinction made between the *finis operis*, whereby all validly baptized persons are baptized *into* the Catholic Church insofar as there is but one valid baptism, and the *finis operantis*. In relation to the obligation to observe the Catholic form of marriage, they are considered bound who are not only baptized *into* the Catholic Church which is the necessary effect of all valid baptism, but only they who are baptized *in* the Catholic Church, i. e., those only are bound to the observance of the Catholic form of marriage who are incorporated formally in the external communion of the Catholic Church.[2]

The phrase "baptized in the Catholic Church" is used in the decree *Ne temere*[3] to distinguish those who are baptized in the Catholic Church as acknowledged members of the Catholic Church and whom accordingly the decree subjects to the observance of the juridical form in view of their Catholic status, from those who are baptized as schismatics or heretics and whom accordingly the decree exempts from the observance of the juridical form in view of the lack of a recognized Catholic status.[4] The legislation of the Code,

[1] Cf. *supra*, p. 13.

[2] Canon 1099, § 1; Cappello, *De Matrimonio*, n. 412; Doheny, *Canonical Procedure in Matrimonial Cases*, p. 662.

[3] S. C. C., decr. *Ne temere*, 2 aug., 1907—*Fontes*, n. 4340.

[4] *AAS*, III (1911), 163-164; Schenk, *The Matrimonial Impediments of Mixed Religion and Disparity of Cult*, p. 103.

like the decree *Ne temere*, binds with the obligation of the canonical form of marriage all those who are baptized in the Catholic Church.[5] The Code, however, admits an exemption to this general rule which exemption was not allowed by the decree *Ne temere*. The Code exempts from the obligation to observe the form those who received baptism in the Catholic Church when they were born of non-Catholic parents and were reared from infancy in heresy, schism, infidelity, or without any religion at all.[6] It will always be important in cases not within the specified exemption to determine whether or not a child is baptized in the Catholic Church, for the baptized individual who did not receive his baptism in the Catholic Church is exempted on that ground also from the obligation to observe the form of marriage unless he was subsequently converted to the faith.[7]

Catholic baptism viewed as a condition in spite of which there is granted the exemption from the form in favor of those baptized as Catholics is only that Catholic baptism which is conferred before the individual is considered an adult.[8] Since, as regards baptism, all are considered adults who enjoy the use of reason,[9] the baptism in order to be deprived by exception of its effect of imposing the obligation to observe the Catholic form of marriage would have to be conferred before the child reaches the use of reason, for once an individual who enjoys the use of reason voluntarily submits to or chooses the Church through Catholic baptism, he is thereafter bound to the Catholic form of marriage.[10]

Article 2. Determination of the Catholic Baptism of Infants

The question now arises as to how one is to determine when the baptism of a child who has not yet reached the use of reason is to be considered baptism in the Catholic Church. All authors agree

[5] Canon 1099, § 1.
[6] Canon 1099, § 2.
[7] Canon 1099, § 2.
[8] Vromant, *De Matrimonio*, p. 176, n. 215.
[9] Canon 745.
[10] Canon 1099, § 1. Cf. Vermeersch-Creusen, *Epitome*, II, n. 344; Payen, *De Matrimonio*, I, n. 1097.

that the intention attending baptism enters into the determination of the Catholic status and external membership acquired in the Catholic Church and distinguishes it from the general effect of every baptism whereby all validly baptized persons can be said to be baptized into the Catholic Church.

The intention determining the Catholic status is that of the following persons in the order mentioned:

1. The intention of the baptized person himself, if that person has the use of reason.

2. The intention of the parents or tutors in the case of those who do not enjoy the use of reason.

3. The intention of the minister.[11]

As regards baptism, therefore, infants, i. e., those who have not yet reached the age of reason,[12] follow the intention of their parents or tutors and are considered as baptized in the Catholic Church or in a sect depending on the intention of their parents or tutors, unless the parents have no intention in the matter, in which case their status is determined according to the intention of the minister of baptism.[13] This right of the parents to determine the Catholic or non-Catholic baptism of their children arises from their role as natural interpreters of the intention of the child who in the age of infancy cannot determine it.[14] The Church respects this natural right of parents even when it is opposed to baptism in the Catholic Church and she never consents to proceed against the will of the parents in the question of baptism and of education until such time as the children can choose for themselves and freely embrace the faith.[15]

The Code itself reflects this position of the Church in the ques-

[11] Cappello, *loc. cit.—Periodica,* XX (1931), 77; Wernz-Vidal, *Ius Canonicum,* V, n. 263; Vermeersch-Creusen, *Epitome,* II, n. 344; Ayrinhac-Lydon, *Marriage Legislation in the New Code of Canon Law,* p. 142, n. 133.

[12] Canon 745, § 2, n. 1.

[13] Payen, *De Matrimonio,* I, n. 1097; Schenk, *The Matrimonial Impediments of Mixed Religion and Disparity of Cult,* pp. 103-115.

[14] St. Thomas Aquinas, *Summa Theologica* (6 vols., Taurini: Marietti, 1932), III^{a}, q. 68, a. 10; II^{a}, II^{ae}, q. 10, a. 12.

[15] Pius XI, litt. encycl. *Divini illius Magistri,* 31 dec. 1929—*AAS,* XXII (1930), 58-60; Bouscaren, *The Canon Law Digest,* I, 337.

tion of infant baptism and, provided that care is taken for their Catholic education, states that the children of infidels or of two schismatics or heretics, or even of two Catholics who have fallen into apostasy, heresy, or schism [16] are baptized licitly only if their parents or tutors, or at least one of them, consents to the baptism; or if the parents, i. e., the father, mother, grandfather and grandmother, or the tutors either are dead, or have lost their right over the children, or are not able to exercise it.[17] The only exception to these restrictive conditions exist in the case when a child is in danger of death and it is prudently foreseen that it will die before it attains the use of reason. Under these circumstances canon 750, § 1 states that the child may be licitly baptized even against the will of its parents.

The baptism that an infant receives will be manifest according to the intention not only of the parents but also of legitimate guardians, because the latter become the legitimate interpreters of the child's intention through the lawful transfer to them of parental authority; [18] and only in defect of such an intention on their part, will the intention of the minister prevail in determining the religious status consequent upon the baptism a child receives.[19] Only in danger of death will the intention of a Catholic minister prevail over the intention of the heretical, schismatic or apostate parents of the child to determine the religious status consequent upon the child's baptism.[20]

In general, therefore, authors concede that the following children are to be considered baptized in the Catholic Church:

1. Infants brought by Catholic parents or guardians to a Catholic minister of baptism.[21]

[16] Canons 750 and 751.

[17] Canon 750, § 2, 1° and 2°.

[18] Canon 750 and 751; Benedictus XIV, ep. *Postremo mense,* 28 febr. 1747, n. 17—*Fontes,* n. 377; Payen, *De Matrimonio,* n. 1097.

[19] Payen, *loc. cit.*

[20] Canon 750; Payen, *De Matrimonio,* II, 1839; Doheny, *Canonical Procedure in Matrimonial Cases,* p. 663.

[21] Cappello, *De Matrimonio,* n. 412; Doheny, *loc. cit.*

2. Infants of Catholic parents baptized in urgent necessity by a Catholic.[22]

3. A child of Catholic parents baptized when in danger of death by a non-Catholic minister.[23]

4. A child of Catholic parents baptized through fraud or deceit or error by a non-Catholic minister when the parents wanted a Catholic minister.[24]

5. A child baptized in danger of death by a Catholic minister of baptism, cleric or lay,[25] even though its parents are non-Catholics, provided that the danger of death is such that death may prudently be presumed to intervene before the child reaches the age of reason.[26]

6. A child of non-Catholic parents baptized licitly according to the norms of canon 750.[27]

7. A child of Catholic parents baptized in danger of death by a non-Catholic minister, e. g., a doctor or a nurse, when the parents want the child baptized in the Catholic Church.[28]

8. A child born of a mixed marriage, contracted with or without the preliminary *cautiones,* when the child is presented to a Catholic minister.[29]

A child, therefore, baptized in any of the foregoing cases is to be considered baptized in the Catholic Church, and consequently bound thereafter to the Catholic form of marriage. An exemption from the obligation to the canonical form obtains, however, if the child was born of non-Catholic parents,[30] and reared from infancy outside the Church.

[22] Cappello, *loc. cit.—Periodica,* XX (1931), 76; Schenk, *The Matrimonial Impediments of Mixed Religion and Disparity of Cult,* pp. 105-106.

[23] Ayrinhac-Lydon, *Marriage Legislation,* p. 143, n. 133.

[24] Cappello, *loc. cit.—Periodica,* XX (1931), 76; Ayrinhac-Lydon, *loc. cit.*; Petrovits, *The New Church Law on Matrimony* (2. ed., Philadelphia: McVey, 1926), n. 277.

[25] Cappello, *loc. cit.—Periodica,* XX (1931), p. 76.

[26] Cappello, *loc. cit.*; Doheny, *loc. cit.*; Payen, *De Matrimonio,* II, n. 1839.

[27] Vermeersch-Creusen, *Epitome,* II, n. 344; Wernz-Vidal, *Ius Canonicum,* V, n. 263; Cappello, *loc. cit.*; Doheny, *loc. cit.*

[28] Cappello, *loc. cit.—Periodica,* XX (1931), 76; Cappello, *De Matrimonio,* n. 412.

[29] Doheny, *loc. cit.*; Ayrinhac, *loc. cit.*

[30] Canon 1099, § 2; cf. *supra,* p. 14.

Article 3. Doubtful Cases

There is no dispute about the religious status of children presented in the cases of the preceding article. There is some disagreement, however, as to the religious status resulting from the baptism of a child of non-Catholic parents who is baptized illicitly in opposition to the law expressed in canons 750 and 751. Doheny [31] states that if the baptism has been conferred illicitly contrary to the provisions of these canons, it appears that the child is still to be considered as baptized in the Catholic Church. He refers in a footnote to Cappello, Wernz-Vidal, and Vlaming in support of his position, but in the references given these authors are more concerned with the imposition on these individuals of the impediment of disparity of cult than in the religious status resulting from the baptism itself and consider the fact of baptism not in itself but in connection with the education of the child from infancy.[32] Thus Cappello himself actually holds the contrary opinion to the effect, namely, that those who are baptized contrary to the prescription of canons 750 and 751 are not to be considered as baptized in the Catholic Church if reared outside the Church.[33] The same is true of Vlaming.[34] Cappello however, does think the question of their status can be considered a *dubium iuris*.[35]

It is difficult to see how the element of education can affect the religious status consequent upon baptism, unless as indicative of the parents' intention, since they are separate notions, and since the baptism will normally occur several years before the child is capable of accepting or rejecting any religious training whatsoever. This is possibly the reason why the majority of canonical writers, discounting the element of education, require some determination of the religious status at the time of the baptism itself. The element of subsequent education is discussed by authors when they try to deter-

[31] Doheny, *op. cit.*, p. 663.

[32] Cappello, *De Matrimonio,* n. 412; Wernz-Vidal, *Ius Canonicum,* V, n. 263; Vlaming, *Praelectiones Iuris Matrimonii* (3. ed., 2 vols., Bussum in Hollandia, Vol. I, 1919; Vol. II, 1921), II, n. 598.

[33] Cappello, *op. cit.*, n. 412.

[34] Vlaming, *loc. cit.*

[35] Cappello, *loc. cit.—Periodica,* XX (1931), 77.

mine the subjection of individuals to the impediment of disparity of cult. This education of the child may result in its conversion after a non-Catholic baptism, and therefore effect its obligation to observe the impediment of disparity of cult [36] and the canonical form of marriage,[37] and it is in this light that the teachings of Cappello, Vlaming and Wernz-Vidal must be considered.

Schenk admits this, but nevertheless teaches that it cannot be urged that those who are baptized against the prescriptions of canons 750 and 751 are to be considered as not baptized in the Catholic Church.[38] The canons, he says, are intended to prevent the danger of perversion, and it is in this sense that such baptisms are prohibited; and the danger of perversion admitted in the canon itself is indicative of the fact that they are to be regarded as baptisms in the Catholic Church.

It seems, however, that the canons tend rather to protect the natural rights of the parents in the training of their infants [39] and that those who are baptized in opposition to the norms of these canons are to be considered as baptized according to the intentions of the parents or tutors, i. e., they are to be considered as being baptized as non-Catholics.[40] It seems inconsistent to teach regard for parental rights on the one hand and to ignore it in so important a matter as the baptism of a child.[41]

Ayrinhac, however, taught that in view of the disputed discussion of the present case, one must wait for an authentic interpretation.[42] It is safe, however, to conclude in practice that because of the extrinsic authority and of strong intrinsic reasons, those chil-

[36] Canon 1070.

[37] Canon 1099, § 1; cf. *supra*, p. 14.

[38] Schenk, *op. cit.*, p. 107.

[39] Cf. *supra*, p. 38; Gasparri, *Tractatus Canonicus de Matrimonio* (ed. nova, 2 vols. in 1, Romae: Typis Polyglottis Vaticanis, 1938), n. 570 (hereafter referred to as *De Matrimonio*).

[40] Vlaming, *Praelectionis Iuris Matrimonii*, n. 598; Vermeersch-Creusen, *Epitome Iuris Canonici*, II, n. 344; Payen, *De Matrimonio*, II, 1079. In n. 1839 Payen states that canonical equity demands that they be considered baptized as non-Catholics, but admits that the question is disputed.

[41] Cf. *supra*, p. 42.

[42] Ayrinhac-Lydon, *op. cit.*, p. 143.

dren of non-Catholics who are baptized in opposition to the prescriptions of canons 750 and 751 cannot be said, even on the basis of the baptism alone, to be held to the canonical form of marriage, and that a marriage contracted by them without the abservance of the canonical form could not be declared null on these grounds. This is true at least because of the doubt existing in the case and in view of the favor which presumptively must be extended the marriage.[43]

Furthermore, if such children were reared from infancy outside the Church, there is no doubt concerning their exemption from the form of marriage, for in such a case, even if the baptism were to be considered a baptism in the Catholic Church, their non-Catholic training from infancy would entail the circumstance for inducing their exemption from the canonical form.[44]

There is also a dispute concerning the religious status resulting from the baptism of a child offered by apostate parents to a Catholic minister when the parents intend that the child be baptized outside the Catholic Church. According to the general norms, it seems that the religious status of such a child would follow in line with the intention of its parents, and accordingly the child would have to be considered as having received a non-Catholic baptism.[45] Cappello holds, however, that in such a case the intention of the parents is of no avail, but he gives no reason in support of his doctrine.[46] Vermeersch-Creusen admit the case is a disputed one.[47]

In practice, therefore, the same is true as in the case considered immediately above, namely, the marriage contracted by a person so baptized could not be declared null if contracted without the canonical form for the reason that in the case there is a doubt of law[48] regarding any established obligation to observe that form on the basis of baptism received; and if the person were reared from infancy outside of the Church, his freedom from the obligation of the

[43] Canon 1014.

[44] Canon 1099, § 2.

[45] Prümmer, *Manuale Theologiae Moralis*, III, n. 754.

[46] Cappello, *loc. cit.—Periodica*, XX (1931), 77.

[47] *Epitome*, n. 344.

[48] Canon 1014.

form is assured for an additional undisputed reason in the very words of canon 1099, § 2.

The case of the baptism of an infant in its mother's womb presents another problem. Such a baptism is doubtful [49] and unless rectified by subsequent conditional baptism in the Catholic Church [50] a person could not clearly be said to be bound to the Catholic form of marriage,[51] and a marriage contracted contrary to the Catholic form could never be declared invalid for lack of the observance of the required canonical form.[52] Once the Catholic baptism were established, however, the child would be thereafter bound to the Catholic form of marriage, unless it were born of non-Catholic parents and reared from infancy outside the Church, in which circumstances it would share the freedom from the obligation of the form allowed by canon 1099, § 2, for just such a case.

49 Canon 746, § 1 and § 5.
50 Canon 746, § 5.
51 Schenk, *op. cit.*, p. 109.
52 Canons 1070, § 2, and 1014.

CHAPTER VI

THE MEANING OF THE PHRASE "AB INFANTILI AETATE" IN CANON 1099, § 2

THERE are juridical norms regarding the factor of age in the Code of Canon Law. These norms entail important consequences. Persons who have reached the age of majority, for example, have the full exercise of their rights, whereas minors in the exercise of their rights remain subject to their parents or tutors except in the cases in which the law exempts them.[1] Among these cases is that which gives a minor the right to acquire a quasi-domicile [2] and the right to choose the Church and cemetery of burial for those who have reached the age of puberty (*puberes*).[3] Infants are said not to be subject to ecclesiastical laws unless the law expressly decrees otherwise,[4] and those who have not attained the status of puberty (*impuberes*) are excused from penalties which are of a *latae sententiae* character.[5] These few examples indicate how important a role the element of age plays in the legislation of the Code, and how much attention must be given it in many important problems.

The norms regarding the factor of age as affecting ecclesiastical legislation are determined in the Code itself. Canon 88 states that a person who has completed his twenty-first year is in his majority and that below this age one is a minor. Minors are presumed to have reached the age of puberty when they have completed their fourteenth year, in the case of boys, or their twelfth year, in the case of girls. They are called *Puberes* in the language of the canon.[6] *Impuberes*, i. e., those who have not yet reached the canonical age of puberty, are presumed to have reached the age of reason when they have com-

[1] Canon 89.

[2] Canon 93, § 1.

[3] Canon 1223, § 2.

[4] Canon 12.

[5] Canon 2230.

[6] Canon 88, § 2.

pleted their seventh year; but before they have completed their seventh year (*ante plenum septennium*) they are presumed not to have the use of reason and are called by the special name of infants (*infans seu puer vel parvulus*).[7] The notion of infancy plays an important role in the correct understanding of canon 1099, § 2.

A necessary condition required to share the exemption of canon 1099, § 2, is that a child, when born of non-Catholics and baptized in the Catholic Church, be reared in heresy or schism or infidelity or without any religion "*ab infantili aetate*." What does the phrase "*ab infantili aetate*" mean? It designates the period up to but exclusive of seven completed years. Canon 88, § 3, states that an *infans* is one who has not yet reached the age of seven completed years. Therefore the adjective *infantili* must indicate that same period of life, namely, the duration of the child's life up to an age exclusive of seven completed years.[8]

Nau (1869-1935) taught that the children considered in the exemption of canon 1099, § 2, are not held to the form of marriage unless they have been educated in the faith after they have arrived at the age of seven years.[9] This conclusion is clearly contrary to the notion of the canon. The notion of the phrase "*ab infantili aetate*" cannot be satisfied after the completion of the seventh year of age; but rather those things which are required to establish the status of a child either as raised in or outside the Catholic Church must be reckoned with not only when they occur after the age of seven years but also when they occur before that time, as is clear from the very words of the canon themselves.[10] It must be admitted that acts of a religious nature before the age of seven completed years do furnish the basis for a judgment whether the child is bound to or exempt from the obligation to observe the canonical form.[11]

[7] Canon 88, § 3.

[8] Allen, "The Test of Catholicity under Canon 1099: Objections Resolved." —*The Jurist*, IV (1944), p. 128.

[9] *Manual on the Marriage Laws of the Code of Canon Law* (2 ed., New York and Cincinnati: Frederick Pustet Company, Inc., 1934), p. 155, n. 123.

[10] Vromant, *Jus Missionariorum*, V, n. 215; Claeys-Bouuaert-Simenon, *Manuale Juris Canonici* (3 vols., Gandae et Leodii: Dessain, Vols. I et III, 3. ed., 1930; Vol. II, 1931), II, n. 304; Cappello, *De Matrimonio*, n. 701.

[11] Marx, *Declaration of Nullity of Marriages Contracted Outside the*

It is readily granted that acts placed by an infant without the use of reason will bear no influence upon its personal acceptance of any religion and that its Catholic or non-Catholic training under such conditions need carry no weight in the judgment regarding its obligation to observe the canonical form of marriage in view of such a personal acceptance of the faith; but the lack of the use of reason in infancy is only a presumption of law and falls before factual proof to the contrary.[12] According to the natural law one without the use of reason is incapable of acting juridically, but once the use of reason has been obtained, a person acquires this capacity.[13]

The Code, however, obviates the difficulty that might arise in determining the age at which reason asserts itself in the child and the time of its subsequent obligation to the laws of the Church by exempting all those who have not completed their seventh year from the obligation of merely ecclesiastical laws even though they have obtained the use of reason, except in those cases where the law expressly decrees otherwise.[14] It is the element of age, however, and not the use of reason that is the determining factor of the concept of infancy in the Code. A person who has not yet completed his seventh year is an infant, even though *de facto* he has obtained the use of reason.[15]

Though ordinarily seven years of age may be required in the individual whose acts are to be taken as manifestations of a personal acceptance of the Catholic faith, this is only due to the presumption of law that after the completion of seven years the age of reason has been obtained. Fundamentally it is the use of reason

Church, The Catholic University of America Canon Law Studies, n. 182 (Washington, D. C.: The Catholic University of America Press, 1943), p. 62; *L'Ami du Clerge,* XLIV (1927), p. 224; Allen, *loc. cit.—The Jurist,* IV (1944), p. 128.

[12] Coronata, *Institutiones Iuris Canonici* (5 vols., Taurini: Marietti, 1928-1936; Vol. IV, *De Delictis et Poenis,* 1935), I, 135, n. 120; Maroto, *Institutiones Iuris Canonici ad Normam Novi Codicis* (2 vols., Vol. I, 3. ed., Romae: Apud Commentarium pro Religiosis, 1921), I, 426; Beste, *Introductio in Codicem* (editio altera, Collegeville, Minn.: St. John's Abbey Press, 1944), p. 134.

[13] Michiels, *Principia Generalia de Personis in Ecclesia* (Lublin: Brasscheat, 1932), p. 32.

[14] Canon 12. Cf. Michiels, *op. cit.*, p. 33.

[15] Canon 88, § 3. Cf. Maroto, *Institutiones Iuris Canonici,* I, n. 429.

itself that is the norm for judging the value of acts. If the use of reason is present in a child before the age of seven, the acts of that child suffice as the basis for the manifestation of the Catholic or non-Catholic training of the individual and of his acceptance of the Catholic faith.[16] If, therefore, the presumption of law that an infant, i. e., one who has not yet completed his seventh year, does not have the use of reason falls before contrary proof, and the infant *de facto* has the use of reason, any religious acts placed by that infant furnish a basis for the determination of his obligation to observe the canonical form of marriage or of his exemption from that form according to the norms of canon 1099, § 2.[17]

That acts performed with the use of reason suffice to establish one's acceptance of the Catholic faith and one's training in that faith regardless of the age of the individual who performs such acts is a solid canonical principle. The Code of Canon Law itself indelibly marks as a Catholic one who performs certain acts after reaching the use of reason. Canon 745, § 2, 2°, states that all those who enjoy the use of reason are adults as far as baptism is concerned, and that they may be baptized at their own request. Anyone, therefore, who has attained the use of reason is considered capable of choosing the Catholic faith through baptism.

Canon 906 obliges all who have attained the use of reason to confess their sins at least once a year. Canon 859, states that all the faithful who have reached the use of reason are obliged to receive the sacrament of the Eucharist once a year, at least at Easter time. In a private reply published in *"Il Monitore Ecclesiastico"* the Commission for the Interpretation of the Code declared that children who have been admitted to first Holy Communion, although they have not completed their seventh year but have reached the age of discretion or the use of reason, are bound by the two precepts of confessing at least once a year and of receiving Holy Communion once a year, at least at Easter time.[18]

[16] Allen, *loc. cit.*—*The Jurist*, IV (1944), 125.

[17] Vromant, *De Matrimonio*, p. 176, n. 215; Marx, *Declaration of Nullity of Marriages Contracted Outside the Church*, p. 62; Cappello, *De Matrimonio*, n. 701.

[18] Bouscaren, *The Canon Law Digest*, I, 53; Canons 854; 859; 906.

Therefore the Code presumes that once a child has the use of reason he is capable of personally accepting or rejecting the faith. All that is required in the child is the use of reason. No one can be found who would deny that a child as considered in canon 1099, § 2, who had gone to confession in accordance with canon 906 and received Holy Communion in accordance with canon 859, would in later life be bound to the canonical form of marriage, even though the sacrament was received before the age of seven. The same can be said of the child who receives Communion in danger of death. All that canon 854, § 2, requires of a child in such circumstances is that it be able to distinguish the Body of Christ from ordinary bread and that it be able reverently to adore the Sacred Presence. Once the child had received Holy Communion under these conditions, he would be bound thereafter to the canonical form of marriage, even though the sacrament were received before the completion of his seventh year of age.[19]

While the religious education to which an infant who does not enjoy the use of reason has been subjected, and the religious acts placed by the child at that time, will not serve as an indication of its personal acceptance of a religious affiliation, they nevertheless constitute part of its religious training. Authors teach that the children of converts, even though baptized in a non-Catholic sect, are to be considered themselves Catholics and bound to the Catholic form of marriage if they do not reject the Catholic training they received upon coming to the use of reason.[20] The same can certainly be said of the *"ab acatholicis nati."* Therefore, if the latter were trained in Catholicism during infancy and accepted the faith upon coming to the use of reason, they cannot be said to have been reared from infancy in heresy or schism or without any religion. They would therefore be bound to the canonical form of marriage. If, however, in consequence of the circumstances of its religious training the child never accepted the Catholic faith upon coming to the use of reason, it would share the exemption from the form of marriage allowed in canon 1099, § 2. The law implies a continuity of non-Catholic belief

[19] Allen, "The Test of Catholicity under Canon 1099: Objections Resolved" —*The Jurist*, IV (1944), 127.

[20] Cf. *infra*, p. 62.

from a period preceding the use of reason through the time when the use of reason was acquired and up to the time of marriage. The child affected by such a state of mind remains a non-Catholic even though it has been baptized in the Catholic Church. Such a case must not be confused with the case of those who knowingly and willingly belonged to the Catholic Church, but later defected from it. The latter would still be bound to the form of marriage.

An objection has been raised to the use of acts of a religious nature performed before the age of seven completed years as a basis for determining the exemption from the obligation to the observance of the canonical form of marriage according to the norms of canon 1099, § 2. It has been objected that no ecclesiastical law binds a baptized person who has not yet completed his seventh year of age. Canon 12 states this fact; but an answer to the objection is found in a more complete study of the canon itself and its relation to the phrase *"ab acatholicis nati"* of canon 1099, § 2.

When canon 12 sets the age of seven completed years as the age at which merely ecclesiastical laws begin to bind baptized persons, it does so with limitation. It states that the age of seven completed years is mandatory for the imposition of the obligation of the law, unless the law in question specifies otherwise or expressly dispenses with that age. Canon 1099, § 2, is such an exception which imposes an obligation to be effective in given cases even before the age of seven completed years. It assumes that in some cases religious acts of a non-Catholic character will be performed by the child and that in others a foundation will be laid for the performance of those acts before the age of seven completed years. In either case it regards as fulfilled the condition of non-Catholic training required to exempt from the obligation to the form of marriage. It states that children born of non-Catholics, even though baptized in the Catholic Church, are not bound to the Catholic form of marriage if they are reared outside the Church from infancy *(ab infantili)*[21] i. e., from that period of life before the seventh completed year has been attained. Canon 1099, § 2, sets aside the general rule of canon 12 by means of the words *"ab infantili aetate,"* an exception such as is allowed

[21] Canon 1099, § 2.

by canon 12 in the very words of the canon itself. Therefore the acts of a religious nature performed before the age of seven years either as an acceptance of a non-Catholic creed or as a preparation for that acceptance, do furnish the basis for deducing an exemption from the obligation to the canonical form as allowed in canon 1099, § 2. If such religious acts are placed by an infant having the use of reason they clearly demonstrate its personal acceptance of a religious affiliation.[22]

Totally to disregard the religious training that a child receives before the completion of its seventh year, and to consider only that training to which it has been subjected after that age, is to fail in fulfilling the requirements of canon 1099, § 2. The canon clearly demands for the exemption from the form allowed to the *"ab acatholicis nati"* that they be reared outside the Church from infancy, that is even before the completion of their seventh year.

[22] Allen, *loc. cit.*; Claeys-Bouuaert-Simenon, *Manuale Juris Canonici,* II, n. 304.

CHAPTER VII

EDUCATION IN THE CATHOLIC CHURCH

Article 1. Lack of Catholic Education a Necessary Condition of Canon 1099, § 2

According to the words of canon 1099, § 2, the condition of the subject's religious training includes two elements: one positive and the other negative. The positive element is the actual foundation which is laid for the acceptance after the attainment of the use of reason of a formal or informal status in some heretical or schismatic sect or in infidelity. Given this positive non-Catholic foundation as operating upon the child from infancy through the age of discretion and resulting in the individual's rearing outside the Catholic Church, he is exempted from the form of marriage provided that the other conditions of the canon are fulfilled. This foundation may be based on an element of positive non-Catholic religious training which, however, is not necessary to induce the exemption. There is also a negative element which suffices to establish the foundation on which the exemption rests. This foundation is equally established if the subject has been reared from infancy without any religion. The phrase "*sine ulla religione*" in canon 1099, § 2, is expressly stated as a negation that suffices to establish this foundation. The Code does not expressly state that the condition expressed in the phrase "*sine ulla religione*" is to be understood as meaning without Catholic training; but, without discussing the point, authors who treat the problems of religious training in relation to the exemption here under consideration often take it for granted that the phrase "*sine ulla religione*" is to be understood as indicating a total lack of training in the Catholic religion.[1]

In practice, however, the meaning of the phrase "*sine ulla religione*" will present no real difficulty. It means without any training

[1] Augustine, *A Commentary on Canon Law,* V, 303; Petrovits, *The New Church Law on Matrimony,* n. 505.

in the Catholic religion or without any training in any religion whatsoever; because once the child is reared from infancy outside the Catholic Church, whether through positive training in a non-Catholic religion, or by a lack of any religious training whatsoever be it Catholic or non-Catholic, the condition of the canon is equally fulfilled. It is the lack of Catholic training that is the essential element and a most important condition postulated for exemption from the form of marriage for the *"ab acatholicis nati."* The exemption presumes that the person born of non-Catholic parents, but baptized in the Catholic Church, never accepted or realized his obligation to or connection with that Church, but was reared from infancy in some other religious belief, or without any religion at all. Once however the person was reared in the Catholic and accepted it as his religious affiliation, he would ever thereafter be held to the Catholic form of marriage.

The difficult question is how much Catholic training is required to effect the Catholic training and education of a child as it is understood in canon 1099, § 2? How much Catholic education is required to bind a child once for all to the canonical form of marriage? When can it be said that a child was reared in the Catholic Church or outside the Catholic Church?

As yet the law has stated no definite rules that afford answers to these questions, and likewise no principles of jurisprudence have been indicated. Early commentators almost entirely ignored the problem, and more recent writers, with few exceptions, have hesitated to contribute norms of particular helpfulness. The difficulties which the present question presents are further increased by the variety of the classes of persons that may emerge in an investigation of practical cases.

In approaching the problem one must never fail to remember that canon 1099, § 2, in the exemption from the form of marriage it allows the *"ab acatholicis nati,"* constitutes an exception to the general rule.. The exceptive rule must therefore be interpreted strictly.[2] Not every semblance of a reason releases those baptized Catholic of non-Catholic parents from the obligation of the Catholic

[2] Canon 19.

form of marriage. The law requires that they grow up from infancy in heresy, or schism or infidelity, or without any religion. It presumes, therefore, that they have been reared outside the Catholic Church. If they have been reared as Catholics, the obligation of the form binds them. If from his infancy the teachings and practices of the Catholic Church were not inculcated in the individual, but he was reared outside the Church, he is not bound to the Catholic form of marriage; [3] but if on the other hand a child was reared from infancy in the Catholic Church and accepted that Church that child cannot be said to have grown up in a sectarian or irreligious atmosphere, and must therefore be considered as a Catholic and forever bound to the Catholic form of marriage, even though he were later to defect from the faith.[4]

In the investigation of the Catholic or non-Catholic training of persons considered in the present discussion, each case will bring difficulties of its own. The party under investigation may have received absolutely no Catholic instruction at all; he may have lived in a non-Catholic atmosphere and not so much as known that he was baptized a Catholic. Such a case will present no difficulty. On the other hand, the investigation may disclose that an individual who at first glance seems to enjoy exemption from the canonical form of marriage was in fact secretly instructed in the Catholic faith by a relative or a friend; or even that he received some catechetical instructions, and that he attended Mass for some time. He may have made a personal study of the Catholic religion and assisted at Catholic functions with friends. The person may have been very intelligent or very dull; he may have assisted frequently at Catholic functions either because he accepted the Church or only for aesthetic purposes.

The individual may be well instructed in the faith or poorly instructed; he may have adhered to the Catholic faith for a long or short period of time, known more or less of the Church's liturgy and her prayers, and followed her teaching with more or less fidelity. Certainly the mere learning of Catholic prayers and Catholic teachings is not sufficient to constitute a Catholic training since many

[3] Canon 1099, § 2; Petrovits, *The New Church Law on Matrimony*, n. 505.

[4] Augustine, *A Commentary on Canon Law*, V, 303.

Catholic prayers are known and used by non-Catholics, and since the mere knowledge of the Church's teaching of itself need be nothing but the indication of one's erudition. Furthermore, there are many poorly instructed Catholics who attend Mass and receive the Sacraments frequently, who would be surprised to be told that they are not Catholics simply in view of their defective knowledge of the truths of Catholicism.

From the above considerations it becomes evident that many factors must be taken into consideration in cases involving the Catholic or non-Catholic training before a decision can be safely reached as to the religious status of the person. There must be added the objective fact of one's Catholic baptism, and the reasonable proof based on objective indications of one's Catholic status. Once this Catholic status is adequately established to have been acquired, it results in the obligation of the individual to observe the canonical form of marriage.[5]

Article 2. Effects of Express and Tacit Acceptance of the Catholic Faith

A. Express Acceptance

There is no one who denies that the element of a personal acceptance of the Catholic Faith by the individual is essential for the acquisition of a Catholic status such as would bind him thereafter to the canonical form of marriage. Oesterle[6] recalls that according to the authors there are two kinds of such a personal acceptance of the faith that result in the acquisition of an objective Catholic status of the individual and in his subsequent obligation to the Church's laws on the form of marriage. The one is some formal or express acceptance of the Catholic Church, as displayed in some formal act of reception into the Church, and the other is a tacit acceptance or profession of the faith as clearly deduced from the person's actions, but without a formal act of reception into the Church, e. g., his attendance at Mass, recitation of Catholic prayers, and his use of Catholic practices, devotions, and such like. Some canonical

[5] Doheny, *Canonical Procedure in Matrimonial Cases*, p. 670.

[6] Casus—*Apollinaris*, XII (1939), 103-109.

writers consider the reception of a sacrament as a formal and express profession and acceptance of the Catholic faith.[7] Others consider it only a tacit acceptance.[8]

Regardless of their disagreement in this classification of the reception of a sacrament, all canonical writers who treat the point agree that the canonical form of marriage binds all those who have made a personal profession of Catholicism in some formal rite of reception into the Church or by the reception of a sacrament. Thus the convert who abjures heresy and embraces the faith is held to the canonical form of marriage even though he were later to defect from the Church. If a child receives the sacrament of penance, or makes his first Holy Communion or can prove his Confirmation, there is no one who will deny his obligation to observe the canonical form of marriage.[9] In all such cases wherein the children born of non-Catholics, as considered in canon 1099, § 2, can be proved to have made their first Holy Communion or to have received a sacrament, there is no doubt that such children are bound to observe the canonical form of marriage even though they later defect from the faith.[10]

B. Tacit Acceptance

In the absence of such a formal profession of faith, or in the lack of the reception of some sacrament after baptism, there is no such unanimity of opinion as to what constitutes the sufficiency of a profession or acceptance of the Catholic faith that is only tacit as fulfilling the requirement of canon 1099, § 2, in the matter of the Catholic training of persons born of non-Catholics and baptized in the Catholic Church. Many authors do not consider the point, but with the increased frequency of practical cases arising, canonical writers are giving the problem more consideration, and the sufficiency

[7] Allen, "The Test of Catholicity under Canon 1099," *The Jurist,* III (1943), p. 600.

[8] Oesterle, *loc. cit.*

[9] Wernz-Vidal, *Ius Canonicum,* V, n. 648; Gasparri, *De Matrimonio,* II, nn. 1020, 1024. Cf. Mahoney, "'*Ab Acatholicis Nati*' (can. 1099, § 2")—*The Clergy Review* (London, 1931 —), XVI (1939), 511-520.

[10] Allen, *loc. cit.—The Jurist,* III (1943), 600.

of a tacit acceptance of Catholicism for inducing the obligation to observe the canonical form of marriage is supported by a preponderance of authors who consider the problem.[11]

By tacit profession and acceptance of the Catholic Church authors mean a personal acceptance verified, not by an explicit, express or formal profession of the faith, as would be demonstrated for example by the reception of a heretic into the Church according to the prescription of the Ritual, but an acceptance of the Church as demonstrated by an individual's personal acts which indicate the acceptance of Catholicism as the choice of his religious affiliation, and which objectively express in themselves the person's subjective Catholic conviction.[12]

Thus, according to this opinion, the attendance at Mass from time to time, the recitation of Catholic prayers, the practice of Catholic devotions, the use of Catholic sacramentals and such like acts and practices suffice to prove a person's Catholic affiliation, even though he has received no sacrament, if at the same time they are the manifestation of a personal, interior acceptance of the Catholic faith and are performed by the person with the intention of professing his Catholic Faith. The intention of professing the Catholic faith, or at least the intention of living according to it, is a necessary requirement demanded by the exponents of the opinion which accepts a tacit acceptance of the Catholic Church as sufficient to fulfill the condition of being reared in the Catholic Church. But no amount of study in Catholic teachings would be accepted as proof of one's Catholic status if the study were made only for the sake of erudition. If a person's attendance at Catholic services is motivated only by his love of the Church's liturgy or for other aesthetic purposes, or if it is prompted by the person's desire to attend Catholic services from time to time only to accompany a friend—there is no one who would see in such practices evidences of an acceptance of the Catholic Church. If, on the other hand, there is even a minimum of such Catholic practice joined with the

[11] Allen, *loc. cit.*—*The Jurist,* III (1943), 601; Beijersbergen, "Casus"—*Periodica,* XXX (1941), 50.

[12] Beijersbergen, *loc. cit.;* Oesterle, *loc. cit.*—*Apollinaris,* XII (1939), 103-109; Triebs, *Handbuch des kanonischen Eherechts,* p. 607.

personal conviction that one is a Catholic, or if this Catholic practice is motivated by a sense of obligation that arises from a person's conviction of his Catholic status, the condition of a total lack of religious training as inducing the exemption of canon 1099, § 2 is not present, even though the person received no other sacrament after baptism. Such a person is therefore bound to the Catholic form of marriage.[13]

Any degree of real Catholic training is enough to render one bound to the form. Canon 1099, § 2, is an exception to the general rule and must therefore be interpreted strictly. Thus the slightest coherence between the Catholic baptism and the Catholic practice will render one bound to the canonical form of marriage, at least if no acceptance of heresy has intervened on the part of the child.[14]

In support of the opinion which considers a tacit acceptance of the Catholic Church as sufficient to oblige the *"ab acatholicis nati"* of canon 1099, § 2, to the canonical form of marriage, it will be of great importance to recall the doctrine of the authors who maintain that such a tacit acceptance of the faith suffices to effect the conversion of those children whose parents themselves have become converted to the faith, even though the children themselves were baptized outside the Catholic Church and provided that the children do not reject the faith from the time they have attained the use of reason until they reach the age of fourteen.[15]

Chelodi [16] teaches that an infant, though baptized in a non-Catholic sect, is presumed converted to the faith if it is reared in the Catholic Church from infancy by its parents who are converted to the Church during the child's infancy, and maintains that the same is true of all those children who are still *impuberes,* i.e, of those children who have completed their seventh year of age but who have

[13] Allen, "The Test of Catholicity under Canon 1099: Objections Resolved" —*The Jurist,* IV (1944), 124; Claeys-Bouuaert-Simenon, *Manuale Juris Canonici,* II, n. 304.

[14] Graneris, "De iis qui sine ulla religione adoleverunt"—*Apollinaris,* XI (1938), 570.

[15] Vermeersch-Creusen, *Epitome* II, n. 344; Farrugia, *De Matrimonio et Causis Matrimonialibus Tractatus Canonico-Moralis Iuxta Codicem Juris Canonici* (Taurini-Romae: Marietti, 1924), n. 238.

[16] *Ius Matrimoniale,* n. 138.

not yet reached the age of puberty,[17] unless these *impuberes* openly oppose the Catholic faith and openly refuse to accept it. Vlaming [18] and Sipos [19] adopt the same teaching, and Payen [20] calls it the more probable opinion. Vidal adds further weight to this opinion and states that the child in such a case is presumed to be converted to the faith even though he lives as a Catholic at least for only some time. Cappello [21] expressly teaches that those children whose parents are converted to the faith are presumed to be converted themselves, even though they were baptized in some non-Catholic sect, and their parents were converted after the children had reached the use of reason, provided that the children grew up in the Catholic faith. He states that even though such children had received some training in heresy or schism before the conversion of their parents, the subsequent training in the Catholic faith effects their conversion and obliges them to the Church laws on the form of marriage.

The above opinion is commonly held by all canonical writers who treat the point and accordingly may be accepted as reflecting a reliable interpretation of the import of the law in question.[22]

In the case of tacit acceptance of the faith it is to be noted that there is required no formal act of reception into the Church. No reception of any of the sacraments after baptism is demanded. All that is required is a tacit acceptance of the faith manifested by the absence of any opposition to the Catholic faith and at least some positive Catholic practice. Given this personal though tacit acceptance of the faith, the child of converted parents, even though it was baptized in a non-Catholic sect, is presumed to be itself a member of the Church even though it was never formally received

[17] Cf. Canon 88, § 3.

[18] *Praelectiones Iuris Matrimonii,* II, n. 598.

[19] *Enchiridion Iuris Canonici,* n. 134.

[20] *De Matrimonio,* II, n. 1840.

[21] Wernz-Vidal, *De Matrimonio,* n. 700.

[22] Gasparri, *De Matrimonio,* n. 1020; Gougnard, *Tractatus de Matrimonio* (7. ed., Mechliniae: Dessain, 1931), p. 214; Allen, *loc. cit.—The Jurist,* III (1943), 600.

into the Church and never received any sacrament after its reception of baptism.[23]

If such a tacit acceptance of the faith suffices to effect the conversion of a child who is baptized outside the Catholic Church, one must concede *a fortiori* that it will suffice as well in the case of the *"ab acatholicis nati"* of canon 1099, § 2. The latter are already members of the Church by baptism. It would be illogical to demand more for their obligation to observe the form of marriage as a result of Catholic training than for the former class who by baptism belong to a non-Catholic sect.

Objection has been taken to the sufficiency of a tacit profession of the faith as effecting conversion to the faith. The objection is based upon the discussion that attends a Rota decision[24] in 1887, handed down in the case of a certain Vladimir who had been baptized at the age of nine in a schismatic sect. During his school years he followed the non-Catholic rite of his father's sect. In the meantime, however, he received some Catholic training from his Catholic mother and, after finishing school, began attending the Catholic Church. In 1906 he left home. In 1917 he married a non-Catholic girl before her minister and according to the rite of her Church. After the marriage Vladimir and his wife returned to the former's childhood home. Just before leaving for military service in World War I, Vladimir and his wife both abjured their schism and were received into the Catholic Church. Upon Vladimir's return from the war,

[23] It has already been determined by the Holy Office that child converts under the age of fourteen years are not obliged to make the abjuration of heresy. In a letter of March 8, 1882 (*Fontes,* n. 1073) this rule as proposed by Cardinal Albizzi (1593-1684), (*De Inconstantia in Fide* [Amstel., 1683], Pars I, cap. XIV, n. 58), is quoted and approved. Cf. Goodwine, *The Reception of Converts,* The Catholic University of America Canon Law studies, n. 198 (Washington, D. C.: The Catholic University of America Press, 1944), p. 122.

[24] S.R.R., *Varsavien., Nullitatis matrimonii,* 10 aug. 1926, coram R.P.D. Francisco Parrillo, Dec. XXXIX—*S. Romanae Rotae Decisiones seu Sententiae* (S.R.R. Dec.), *quae prodierunt anno 1926 cura eiusdem S. Tribunalis editae* (Romae: Typis Polyglottis Vaticanis, 1935), XVIII (1926), 3130318. Decisions of the Sacred Roman Rota which were made from 1909 onward were published from 1912 onward. The collection is hereafter referred to as *S.R.R. Dec.*

his marriage turned out unhappily and he petitioned for a declaration of nullity of the marriage on the grounds of a lack of the proper observance of the requisite form. He based his claim upon his obligation to the Catholic form of marriage that resulted from the Catholic training he had reecived from his mother and from his attendance at services in the Catholic Church.

In its discussion of the case, the appointed panel of the Rota stated that conversion to the Catholic faith could not be deduced from a private manner of acting but only from some act performed according to the rite of the Catholic Church which carried with it enrollment in the Catholic Church. It said it doubted that children who had been baptized as non-Catholics but whose parents were afterwards converted to the Faith, could themselves be considered converted simply in view of a Catholic education. It conceded on the latter point, however, that there were authors who held the contrary opinion. The panel concluded that Vladimir could not expect to have his marriage declared null as a result of his obligation to deserve the Catholic form of marriage, and in view of his failure to observe that form in contracting the marriage. The conversion to the faith which as he claimed occurred prior to his marriage could not, it continued, be effected by means of his participation in the divine offices and his frequentation of the Catholic Church, but would have required some rite or ritual ceremony in the Church. As a result of its argumentation, the Rota decided that Vladimir's marriage could not be declared null *ex defectu formae* inasfar as he had not been converted to the Catholic Church prior to his marriage and was therefore not obliged to observe the Catholic form of marriage as determined in the decree *Ne temere* which was in force at the time when the marriage was contracted.

There are some interesting facts, however, revealed in a closer study of the above case that seem to make an answer to the objection not too difficult. It is first of all an isolated case, and does not of itself suffice to establish a practice of the Roman Curia. Moreover though the panel of the Rota expressly opposed those authors who taught that a tacit acceptance of the faith by children whose parents were converted sufficed to effect the conversion of the children it did so with some hesitancy; furthermore there is great weight of authority against the Rota's view even by authors who make special mention of the case in which this view was expressed.[25]

The case history of Vladimir in itself lacks elements required by the authors as necessary to effect conversion, and the Rota seems to have based its decision more upon these than upon its opinion that such a conversion was not possible. Vladimir was baptized as an adult. He knowingly and voluntarily submitted to his baptism in a schismatic sect. He followed that sect for some years. In spite of his attendance at the Catholic Church, he married a non-Catholic girl in her rite and before her minister. Finally, on his return home he formally abjured his heresy and entered the Catholic Church. All of these were strong indications that Vladimir had never made an acceptance of the Church before his marriage—an element required by all the authors who teach the sufficiency of a tacit acceptance as effecting an individual's conversion. This seems clear from Vladimir's formal entry into the Church after his marriage had taken place; it was evident that he had never really considered himself a Catholic before that time. It was this lack of a personal acceptance of the faith more than his attendance at Catholic services that seemed to influence the decision of the Rota. Again, the authors who adopt the theory of tacit acceptance require for the tacit conversion of the child that he do nothing to contradict his Catholic training before the age of fourteen; but Vladimir had actually been baptized when he was nine years old, and thereupon followed the non-Catholic sect of his father until his entire schooling was completed. One must admit, however, that while many statements set down by the Rota in its treatment of this case are perfectly compatible with the opinion that a tacit acceptance of the Church suffices to effect the conversion of children, the fact still remains that it clearly expressed its doubt concerning the opinion. Nonetheless, in view of the great weight of authority that supports the opinion, it seems that one must concede that such a tacit acceptance of the faith does result in the conversion of the children of converts, provided that the children do nothing to contradict that faith before the age of fourteen.[26]

[25] Oesterle, *loc. cit.—Apollinaris,* XII (1939), 103-109.

[26] Cf. *supra,* p. 62; Gougnard, *Tractatus de Matrimonio,* p. 214.

It follows, therefore, that such a tacit acceptance of the faith should fulfill the requirement of a Catholic training sufficient to oblige the *"ab acatholicis nati"* of canon 1099, § 2, to the canonical form of marriage, even though after the baptism no sacrament has been received. If a child, therefore, born of non-Catholic parents, but baptized in the Catholic Church, is reared from infancy in the Catholic Church, even though he has received no other sacrament, he does not share the exemption from the canonical form allowed in canon 1099, § 2, because he can neither be said to have been reared in heresy, in schism or in infidelity nor can he be said to have been reared without any religion. Having thus fulfilled neither of the conditions of positive or negative religious training outside the Catholic Church as required by the canon to induce the exemption from the obligation to observe the canonical form of marriage, he cannot share that exemption.[27]

It is moreover, arbitrary in a sense to say that the reception of a sacrament is required in proof of one's Catholic training which in itself suffices to induce the obligation to observe the form of marriage imposed in canon 1099, § 2. The Code nowhere defines the requisites of a Catholic training or education that at best is only implicitly required of the *"ab acatholicis nati"* for the sake of establishing the Catholic status which suffices to oblige them to the observance of the form of marriage. Catholic training or education is something composite and variable. A perfect Catholic education would be found in one who was well instructed in the teachings of the Church and both publicly and privately diligent in the practices of the faith. But certainly there are degrees of Catholic education. Even though a person were not very well instructed and not very faithful in the practice of his religion, it could not therefore immediately be said that he grew up in heresy or without any religion.

If one imagines the case of a child born of non-Catholic parents but baptized in the Catholic Church, which child was reared from infancy in a heretical sect and who practiced that sect without any training in the Catholic faith, one has in mind a child whose case clearly fulfills the conditions of canon 1099, § 2, and as a result cer-

[27] Canon 1099, § 2.

tainly implies an exemption from the Catholic form of marriage. If the same child had been reared from infancy without any religion at all, his case would again fulfill the condition of the canon and thereby free him from the obligation of observing the form of marriage. Neither of these cases, however, can be identified with a mere negligent or less perfect Catholic education or Catholic mode of life. In the latter case there is no training in heresy or schism. There is no total lack of training in religion. Accordingly the conditions of canon 1099, § 2, are not fulfilled. The case reveals but a poor Catholic training, but nonetheless whatever training attended the case was a Catholic training.

In support of this doctrine Graneris [28] proposes a case in which he decides that Titus, who had been born of a mixed marriage and baptized in the Catholic Church, was bound to the Catholic form of marriage even though he had not made his first Communion, and after his baptism had received no other sacrament. Titus had, however, gone to Mass on such important feast days as Christmas and Easter, considered himself a Catholic, and never attended any other Church. The writer based his decision upon Titus's failure to fulfill the conditions of canon 1099, § 2. The canon exempts the *"ab acatholicis nati"* provided that they were reared from infancy in heresy, or schism, or infidelity or without any religion. Titus, Graneris concludes, fulfills none of these conditions. Titus could not be said to have been reared without any religion because of his religious convictions and occasional religious practice. Neither could he be said to have been reared in heresy or schism since he had never associated himself with either. Graneris concludes from this case the principle that even a minimum of Catholic acts suffices to induce an obligation to the form of marriage in the case of the *"ab acatholicis nati"* provided that they are placed without any simultaneous intermingling of non-Catholic practices.

It is not infrequent that persons are found who were born of a mixed marriage, were baptized in the Catholic Church, and then reached the time of their marriage without having made their first Communion or received any other sacrament. Such people are

[28] "De iis qui sine ulla religione adoleverunt,"—*Apollinaris,* XI (1938), 568-571.

nevertheless absolutely certain of their Catholic status and are recognized as Catholic by their associates. They may have attended Mass at times, or even frequented a Catholic school for a year or two, but have not shown enough interest in doctrine to prepare sufficiently for the reception of the sacraments. It is not uncommon that families in country districts are denied the advantages of frequent Mass or regular catechetical instruction, and yet the children of such families receive some instruction in Catholic teaching and Catholic practice, and accordingly consider themselves Catholics, and are also recognized as such by others. Certainly in such cases as these there is no complete lack of religious training. There is no training in heresy or schism. It is such a tacit acceptance as this that the authors advocate as sufficient to oblige the *"ab acatholicis nati"* to the Catholic form of marriage: namely, a minimum of Catholic education supported by a personal acceptance of Catholicism.[29]

It is safe therefore to conclude that the *"ab acatholicis nati"* of canon 1099, § 2, are not obliged to observe the canonical form provided that:

1. They were reared from infancy in heresy, in schism, or in infidelity, with a total lack of Catholic training.

2. They were reared from infancy without any religious training whatsoever.

They are bound to the form, however, if:

1. They were reared from infancy in the Catholic Church and have received some sacraments after baptism, e.g., first Holy Communion. Their obligation to the form would be sustained in this case even though there were some evidences of heretical training.

2. They have received a minimum of Catholic training from infancy, even though they received no sacrament after baptism, provided that there was a total lack of heretical training.

Greater difficulties will arise when the investigation of practical cases discloses that the persons considered in canon 1099, § 2, were subjected to training both in the Catholic religion and also

[29] Graneris, *loc. cit.;* Vromant, *De Matrimonio,* n. 217; Beijersbergen, "Casus"—*Periodica,* XXX (1941), 46-51; Claeys-Bouuaert-Simenon, *Manuale Juris Canonici,* II, 304.

in some heretical sect. In such cases it must be established that the Catholic training prevailed and that the training in heresy was ineffectual in order that persons concerned may be considered bound to the Catholic form of marriage. In practical cases involving simultaneous training in both Catholicism and in heresy, authors have offered norms indicative of that training in the Catholic Church which suffices to establish a Catholic status sufficient to bind such persons to the form of marriage. Thus it is taught that if the child has had four [80] or even two years of Catholic religious instruction either at school or privately at home, it is safe to conclude that such a child has received a Catholic education and is bound to the form of marriage.[81] One can even safely say that one year at a Catholic school, or any Catholic education equivalent to that, would suffice to bind the child thereafter to the form of marriage if this attendance at school indicated one's claim to a Catholic affiliation. This would seem true even if during that time the child practiced the faith but imperfectly, as long as he practiced it and willingly and knowingly accepted it as his own.

Practical cases of this kind that arise in diocesan tribunals will demand careful scrutiny. If the person has received some sacrament, the solution will be easy enough. All agree that this person is bound to the Catholic form of marriage. Therefore, if a petition for nullity were submitted to the Ordinary by such a person when he had failed to contract marriage according to the canonical formalities, the case could be settled by the Ordinary himself, or by the pastor after consulting the Ordinary, without the necessity of a formal trial.[82]

In cases, however, when the fact of the reception of some sacrament cannot be established or is clearly lacking, it will be necessary to establish the individual's obligation to the form through other proofs of his Catholic education. If sufficient proof cannot be

[80] Allen, "The Test of Catholicity under Canon 1099"—*The Jurist,* III (1943), 601.

[81] Marx, *The Declaration of Nullity of Marriages Contracted Outside the Church,* p. 84.

[82] S. C. de Sacr., instr., 15 aug. 1936—*AAS* XXVIII (1936), 313-361. Cf. art. 231—*Ibid.,* p. 359.

attained though the informal process, and if the person's obligation to the form remains doubtful, a formal process will be necessary.[33] It is taught that the formal process will always be required when the reception of a sacrament has not occurred in the Catholic education of an individual considered in canon 1099, § 2.[34] As long as there remains any positive doubt in practical cases, this is certainly the only safe practice to follow.[35]

[33] Art. 231, § 2—*AAS*, XXVIII (1936), 359.

[34] Hannan, "Validity of Marriage. Canons 1099 and 1070"—*The Ecclesiastical Review*, CIX (1943), 456; Marx, *The Declaration of Nullity of Marriages Contracted Outside the Church*, p. 97.

[35] Marx, *op. cit.*, p. 97.

CHAPTER VIII

MARRIAGES OF PERSONS BORN OF NON-CATHOLICS ("*AB ACATHOLICIS NATI*") WITH PERSONS EXEMPT FROM THE FORM

Article 1. Marriages of Persons Born of Non-Catholics ("*Ab Acatholicis Nati*") with Non-Catholics

Non-Catholics whether baptized or not baptized, are exempt from the obligation to observe the canonical form in contracting marriage provided that they marry among themselves.[1] However, they are indirectly bound to observe the canonical form whenever they contract marriage with persons who are bound to the form.[2]

A marriage contracted between a person baptized in the Catholic Church, or converted to it from heresy or schism, and a person who is a non-Catholic is invalid if contracted without the observance of the formalities required according to canons 1094, 1095, and 1096. Those baptized Catholics, however, who were born of non-Catholic parents and were reared from infancy in heresy in schism in infidelity or without any religion at all are released from the obligation of observing the canonical form of marriage whenever they contract marriage with non-Catholics,[3] i.e., whenever they contract marriage with persons who are not baptized, or who were baptized in a non-Catholic sect but never were converted to the Catholic faith.[4]

Article 2. Marriages of Persons Born of Non-Catholics ("*Ab Acatholicis Nati*") with Orientals

Catholics of the various Oriental rites are not bound by the ecclesiastical laws of the Code unless these laws expressly mention them, or unless of their very nature the laws subject all Catholics alike.[5] The legislation on the juridical form of marriage does not

[1] Canon 1099, § 2.

[2] Canon 1099, § 1, 2°.

[3] Canon 1099, § 2.

[4] Canon 1099, § 1, 1°; § 2.

[5] Canon 1.

embrace the subjects of the Oriental Church, for they are not expressly included under it; but if Catholic Orientals marry Catholics of the Latin rite they are bound to observe the Latin form of the Code.[6]

In the mind of the Church, however, heretics and schismatics of Oriental rites in regard to the form of marriage are included under the term "non-Catholics," so that a person who is born of heretical or schismatical Orientals can be said to be born *"ab acatholicis."* [7] This, of course, would not occasion any practical implication in the light of canon 1099, § 2, unless a child born of non-Catholic Orientals were legitimately baptized in the Latin rite, thus legitimately becoming a member of the Latin rite, and therefore subject to its laws.[8]

What of those marriages contracted without the observance of the form between the *"ab acatholicis nati"* as mentioned in canon 1099, § 2, and Catholic Orientals who are not bound by any form? Are such marriages valid?

The law extends its exemption from the observance of the canonical form only to such marriages as are contracted between the *"ab acatholicis nati"* and non-Catholics (*quoties cum parte acatholica contraxerint*).[9] Many authors however see in the canon a release from the observance of the canonical form as allowed also to the *"ab catholicis nati"* whenever they contract marriage with persons who are themselves free from the observance of any form.[10] While this opinion seems to militate against the literal meaning of the law, it was considered to be solidly probable even by early commentators and to be safe in practice.[11]

This view is supported in a reply given on July 9, 1942, to the

[6] Canon 1 and 1099; cf. Ayrinhac-Lydon, *Marriage Legislation in the New Code of Canon Law*, p. 268.

[7] S.C.C., *Romana et Aliarum*, 28 mart. 1908, ad I et II—*Fontes*, n. 4349; *ASS*, XLI (1908), 288.

[8] Canons 98; 751; 756.

[9] Canon 1099, § 2.

[10] Rossi, *De Matrimonii Celebratione Iuxta Codicem Juris Canonici*, n. 44; Cappello, *De Matrimonio*, n. 701.

[11] Cerato, *Matrimonium a Codice Iuris Canonici Integre Desumptum*, n. 96; Payen, *De Matrimonio*, II, n. 1843; III, n. 1845; Vromant, *Ius Missionariorum*, V, n. 217.

Apostolic Delegate in the United States of America. The Sacred Congregation for the Orientals decided that the *"ab acatholicis nati"* are not bound to the canonical form for the validity of marriage when they contract with Catholics of the Oriental rite who are not bound to any form for the contracting of a valid marriage.[12]

ARTICLE 3. INTER-MARRIAGE OF PERSONS BORN OF NON-CATHOLICS (*"Ab Acatholicis Nati"*)

Persons baptized in the Catholic Church but born of non-Catholic parents, or of whom one at least is a non-Catholic,[13] and who are reared outside the Church, are, in the language of the law, released from the observance of the canonical form of marriage *"quoties cum parte acatholica contraxerint."* [14] Are such persons released from the obligation to the form when they marry among themselves? The solution to this question hinges on the interpretation of the words *"cum parte acatholica"* of the canon.

Augustine [15] thought that the wording of the canon was to be taken in a strict sense. The Code, he said, wishes to restrict the freedom of the *"ab acatholicis nati"* to the sole cases in which they marry those who never belonged nor now belong to the Catholic Church, regardless of whether they were baptized or not, otherwise the law would have expressly made other provisions. Many authors, however, see in the canon a release from the observance of the form allowed to the *"ab acatholicis nati"* whenever they contract marriage with persons who are themselves free from the observance of any form.[16] It was in accord with this opinion that the Sacred Con-

[12] The Most Reverend Apostolic Delegate in the United States forwarded this question to the Sacred Congregation: D. Utrum, firmo praescripto can. 1099, § 1, 1°, ab acatholicis nati, etsi in ecclesia baptizati, qui ab infantili aetate in haeresi vel schismate aut infidelitate vel sine ulla religione adoleverunt, forma canonica pro validitate matrimonii teneantur quoties cum fidelibus ritus orientalis contrahant, qui nulla forma adstringuntur ad validas nuptias ineundas.—R. Negative.—Bouscaren, *Canon Law Digest,* II, 338. Cf. *The Jurist,* II (1942), 399.

[13] Cf. *supra,* p. 22.

[14] Canon 1099, § 2.

[15] *A Commentary on Canon Law,* V, p. 443.

[16] Rossi, *De Matrimonii Celebratione,* n. 44.

gregation for the Orientals decided in 1942 that the persons mentioned in canon 1099, § 2, are not bound to the canonical form of marriage when they contract marriage with Catholic Orientals who are not bound to any form for contracting marriage validly.[17]

Cappello even paraphrases the words of the canon and teaches that they are not obliged to the form *"si contrahant cum iis qui non sunt subiecti formae."* [18] Exponents of this opinion teach that as far as the law regarding the form of marriage is concerned, the *"ab acatholicis nati"* are to be considered as non-Catholics.[19] Consequently they are free from the observance of the form when they marry among themselves.[20] Even authors who consider the question doubtful admit that the opinion is solidly probable and safe in practice.[21]

In fact the great weight of extrinsic authority, the strong probability that the *"ab acatholicis nati"* are included intrinsically under the phrase *"cum parte acatholica"* as regards the form of marriage, and the mind of the Church as expressed in the decision of the Sacred Congregation for the Orientals, incline one to accept it as the more probable and safer opinion. If one wishes to maintain that the *"ab acatholicis nati"* are not included under the phrase *"cum parte acatholica"* as regards the form of marriage, and that the words of canon 1099, § 2, seem to oppose the validity of a marriage contracted without the form between two persons as considered in the canon, then it seems that one must admit that there exists at least a doubt of law and that such a marriage should be held as valid.[22] Until such a time as the Holy See decrees some definite norm, it would certainly be unsound in practice to declare such a marriage null.

[17] Cf. *supra,* p. 72.

[18] *De Matrimonio,* n. 701.

[19] Gasparri, *De Matrimonio,* n. 1042; Wernz-Vidal, *Ius Canonicum,* V, n. 552; Marx, *The Declaration of Nullity of Marriages Contracted Outside the Church,* p. 59.

[20] Fourneret, *Le Mariage Chrétien* (5. ed., Paris: Gabriel Beauchesne, 1925), p. 150; Cerato, *Matrimonium a Codice Iuris Canonici Integre Desumptum,* n. 96.

[21] Payen, *De Matrimonio,* II, 1843; De Smet, *Tractatus Theologico-Canonicus De Sponsalibus et Matrimonio,* n. 143.

[22] Vromant, *De Matrimonio,* n. 217; Canons 15 and 1014; "A Case of Exemption from the Canonical Form of Marriage,"—*The Ecclesiastical Review,* LXXXII (1930), 507-508.

CHAPTER IX

PERSONS BORN OF NON-CATHOLICS OF CANON 1099, § 2 AND THEIR SUBJECTION TO CHURCH LAWS

Article 1. In General

The *"ab acatholicis nati,"* unless expressly exempt, are subject to Church laws. With the reception of baptism, an individual receives a personality in the Church with all the rights and offices of a Christian, unless, as regards his rights, there is some obstacle in the way that impedes his communion with the Church, or he is subject to some censure that deprives him of these rights.[1] Thus it is that all validly baptized persons are bound to the Church's laws unless they are expressly exempt.

This[2] is true not only of Catholics, but it is true of those baptized outside the Church as well. Since the publication of the Code of Canon Law authors have unanimously held to the fundamental subjection of heretics and schismatics to all ecclesiastical laws.[3] The principal season offered by most of them is the reception of the indelible mark of baptism, which makes one a permanent subject of the Church, and bound by all its laws, a reason that is clearly embodied in the rulings of canons 2 and 87 just referred to.[4]

Canon 87 clearly states that baptism gives an individual a juridic personality in the Church and endows him with the rights and offices of a Christian; and canon 12 subjects all baptized persons to ecclesiastical laws unless they do not enjoy the use of reason, or even when they enjoy the use of reason if they have not completed their seventh year. Such is the norm unless the law makes other

[1] Canon 87.

[2] Canons 12 and 13.

[3] Augustine, *A Commentary on Canon Law,* I, n. 87; Maroto, *Institutiones Iuris Canonici ad Normam Novi Codicis,* I, n. 426.

[4] Michiels, *Normae Generales Iuris Canonici* (2 vols., Lublin: Universitas Catholica, 1929), I, 286 (hereafter cited *Normae Generales*).

provisions. Nowhere in the law is there a general provision exempting heretics and schismatics from ecclesiastical laws; therefore they are bound by them. After admitting this general principle of the fundamental subjection of heretics to ecclesiastical laws, many post-Code writers make the same distinctions as were proposed prior to the promulgation of the Code.

All agree that heretics are bound by those laws which pertain to the preserving of public order, or the safeguarding of the ecclesiastical community, or also the laws which are conducive to the public good.[5] Concerning those ecclesiastical laws however that tend primarily to the securing of man's personal sanctification, such as the laws that regulate fast and abstinence, the observance of feasts, or the prohibition of books, there is a difference of opinion.

There are those who teach that the Church, foreseeing the contumacy of heretics and their actual violation of these laws, is presumed to act more mildly in these matters, and accordingly does not wish to oblige them and thus occasion the multiplying of their sins.[6]

While some authors defend the doctrine that heretics are not directly exempt from laws looking to a Christian's personal sanctification, yet they claim exemption from these laws on the part of non-Catholics as an indirect consequence (*per accidens*).[7]

Among these laws that are intended for personal sanctification are to be included those ecclesiastical laws which prescribe certain determined acts for the subjects of the Church, but which non-Catholics are prohibited from performing e. g. the laws of annual confession, of the Pascal Communion, as well as the law that obliges subjects to the hearing of Mass on Sundays and holy days of obligation. While these examples are not classed strictly as ecclesiastical laws, since they are based very directly of the divine law, they are nonetheless ecclesiastical insofar as the Church has determined the exact times at which these divine laws are to be obeyed. Insofar,

[5] Cicognani, *Commentarium ad Librum I Codicis* (Romae: ex Schola Typographia "Pii X," 1925), p. 95; Claeyus Bouuaert-Simenon, *Manuale Juris Canonici,* I, n. 91.

[6] Bargilliat, *Praelectiones Juris Canonici* (37. ed. 2 vols., Parisiis: apud Baston, Berch et Pogis), I, 63.

[7] Cf. Cicognani, *Commentarium ad I Librum Codicis,* p. 95.

then, as they are ecclesiastical laws, the milder opinion, which is safe in practice, frees heretics from their observance.

Other authors while admitting the probability of the foregoing opinion, attack it for various reasons.[8]

The authors say nothing in particular concerning the *"ab acatholicis nati"* and their general subjection to Church law. Certainly by their Catholic baptism they are subjected fundamentally to all Church laws; but it seems reasonable to say that if they are reared from infancy outside the Church they seem to be entitled to the same concessions under the considerations applied to those heretics who are baptized outside the Catholic Church in regard to those ecclesiastical laws that tend primarily to a Christian's personal sanctification. Regardless of what one will maintain on this disputed point, it must be noted that, while the *"ab acatholicis nati"* are indisputably exempt from the observance of the form of marriage, they are subject to the Church's other laws on marriage, such as, for example the law on espousals and the legislation concerning matrimonial impediments. In relation to the latter, however, the Church's law does imply in a specific manner that the impediment of disparity of worship binds only those who were baptized in the Catholic Church, or who were converted to the Church from heresy or schism.[9]

Article 2. Persons Born of Non-Catholics (*"ab Acatholicis Nati"*) of Canon 1099, § 2 in Relation to the Impediment of Disparity of Cult

As regards the question as to whether or not the impediment of disparity of worship is binding upon those who were born of non-Catholic parents and baptized in the Catholic Church, but were reared from infancy outside the Church, there was until recently no unanimity of opinion. The problem was not without its foundation, because though baptized in the Catholic Church, the *"ab acatholicis*

[8] Cance, *Le Code de Droit Canonique* (16. ed., 3 vols., Paris: J. Cabalda et Fils, 1930), I, 49, n. 41; Michiels, *Normae Generales,* I, 289, 290. Cf. McCloskey, "Post-Code Opinions on the Obligation of Heretics to Observe Ecclesiastical Laws"—*The Jurist,* III (1943) p. 480-492.

[9] Canon 1070, § 1.

nati" of canon 1099, § 2, were, at least in regard to the form of marriage, likened to those who were not baptized in the Catholic Church and who accordingly were not bound to the impediment. The question was: Could the similarity to those not baptized in the Catholic Church be extended to the impediment of disparity of worship and did the persons mentioned in canon 1099, § 2, share in the exemption of non-Catholics from the impediment similarly as they shared in the exemption from the form of marriage? In other words, was a marriage when contracted between a person born of non-Catholic parents and baptized in the Catholic Church, but reared from infancy outside the Church, and a non-baptized person valid if it was contracted without a dispensation from the impediment of disparity of worship? Intrinsically it seemed clear that the "*ab acatholicis nati*" were bound to observe the impediment of disparity of cult. Canon 1070 stated that a marriage was null when contracted between a non-baptized person and a person baptized in the Catholic Church or converted to it from heresy or schism. Either baptism or conversion to the Catholic Church sufficed to bind a person to the impediment of disparity of worship. The "*ab acatholicis nati*" of canon 1099, § 2, when baptized in the Catholic Church seemed clearly bound by the impediment. The exemption from the form that they enjoyed when the conditions of the canon were fulfilled did not seem to suffice as a claim to exemption from the impediment of disparity of worship. Canon 1070 did not contain any such exemption in stating the norms for subjection to the impediment, and canon 1099, § 2, was concerned only with the exemption from the form of marriage. This seemed evident not only from the wording of the present Code legislation, but from the history of the law now embodied in canon 1099, § 2, which exempted such persons only from the form, though it was enacted at a time when all baptized persons were subject to the impediment of disparity of worship whether they were baptized in or outside the Catholic Church.[10]

From these considerations it could have been clearly deduced that there was no foundation for any attempt to extend their exemption from the observance of the form of marriage to freedom from sub-

[10] S.C.S. Off., litt. (ad Ep. Harlemen.), 6 apr. 1859—*Fontes*, n. 950.

jection to the impediment of disparity of worship, especially since according to the words of canon 1070 they seemed to be clearly excluded from such exemption in view of their baptism in the Catholic Church. In the case of those born of non-Catholic parents who were not baptized in the Catholic Church or never converted to it, it was clear from canon 1070 itself that there was no subjection to the impediment; but once the fact of Catholic baptism entered the case, they seemed bound even though they were never reared in the Church.[11] Such was the case of the *"ab acatholicis nati"* of canon 1099, § 2.

Nonetheless the question was discussed among canonical writers with uncertainty. Some held that the impediment bound the *"ab acatholicis nati"* of canon 1099, § 2.[12] Others considered the matter doubtful.[13] Therefore, in spite of the intrinsic arguments that seemed to bind the *"ab acatholicis nati"* of canon 1099, § 2, to the impediment of disparity of worship, the doubts that existed at least in the light of extrinsic authority were such as to cause difficulty in practical cases.

Even though one might have been convinced that the *"ab acatholicis nati"* were bound to the impediment, it would have been unsound, in the face of this extrinsic authority, to declare a marriage invalid in consequence of the impediment of disparity of worship, for which no dispensation had been granted, whenever there was question of a marriage contracted by them with the non-baptized. This was true in the light of the principle of canon 1014, *"in dubio standum pro valore matrimonii."* [14]

The doubt that existed in the matter was definitely resolved by

[11] Cappello, *De Matrimonio,* n. 412.

[12] Cerato, *Matrimonium a C.I.C. Integre Sumptum,* p. 88, n. 65; Vlaming, *Praelectiones Iuris Matrimonii,* I, n. 289; Payen, *De Matrimonio,* I, n. 1104; Schenk, *The Matrimonial Impediments of Mixed Religion and Disparity of Cult,* p. 154.

[13] Cappello, *De Matrimonio,* n. 412; Wernz-Vidal, *Ius Canonicum,* V. n. 263; Vermeersch-Creusen, *Epitome,* II, n. 344. Cf. "Exemption from the canonical form of marriage and from disparity of cult," *The Ecclesiastical Review,* LXXXVI (1932), 79-82.

[14] Hannan, "Validity of Marriage. Canons 1099 and 1070."—*The Ecclesiastical Review,* CIX (1943), 453-456.

a decision of the Pontifical Commission for the Authentic Interpretation of the Code. The Commission was asked: "Whether persons born of non-Catholics, mentioned in canon 1099, § 2, are bound, according to canon 1070, by the impediment of disparity of cult when they contract marriage with an unbaptized person?" The reply was: "In the affirmative." [15]

One must admit, then, that those who were born of non-Catholic parents, even though they were reared from infancy outside the Catholic Church, are bound to the impediment of disparity of worship if they received baptism in the Catholic Church. Accordingly a marriage contracted by any such person with an un-baptized person would be invalid unless a dispensation had been obtained from the impediment of disparity of worship to which every person is subject when he has received a Catholic baptism.

Article 3. Persons Born of Non-Catholics ("*Ab Acatholicis Nati*") Released from the Formalities of Canon 1098 and Canons 1133-1137

As far as the Church law regarding the form of marriage is concerned, children born of parents of whom one is a Catholic, the other a non-Catholic or an apostate, or of whom both are non-Catholics or apostates, are, even if they are baptized in the Catholic Church but have received no Catholic education, assimilated to non-Catholics, and are exempt from the praescriptions of canon 1094, which determine the canonical form of marriage. Are they likewise exempt from the obligations of canon 1098? This canon prescribes certain emergency measures that suffice for validity in the contracting of a marriage when there is danger of death or when it is foreseen that the ordinary or the pastor cannot be reached within a month.[16]

[15] Pont. Comm. Intr. 29 apr. 1940—*AAS*, XXXII (1940), 212; Bouscaren, *The Canon Law Digest*, II, 290.

[16] Canon 1098.—Si haberi vel adiri nequeat sine gravi incommodo parochus vel Ordinarius vel sacerdos delegatus qui matrimonio assistant ad normam canonum 1095, 1096:

1°. In mortis periculo validum et licitum est matrimonium contratum coram solis testibus; et etiam extra mortis periculum, dummodo prudenter praevideatur eam rerum conditionem esse per mensem duraturam;

While canon 1098 does not prescribe the full formalities as established in canon 1094, it does prescribe a Catholic form of marriage which, if possible of execution, is necessary for the validity of a marriage.[17] But canon 1099, § 2, excuses the *"ab acatholicis nati"* from the observance of the Catholic form of marriage. It states with regard to them "nullibi tenentur as catholicam matrimonii formam servandam." Therefore they may be said to be excused from the obligations of canon 1098.

Article 4. Convalidation of Marriages of the *"Ab Acatholicis Nati"*

The Church has determined certain formalities in the renewal of consent for the convalidation of a marriage which by the intervention of her law disqualify the parties from obtaining the juridic effects of their consent unless these formalities are observed.[18] These formalities are required by merely ecclesiastical law.[19]

Cappello teaches that these formalities required in the convalidation of marriage are, in fact, reducible to the form of marriage, and that those persons who are released from the obligation of observing the form of marriage are also released from the obligation of the ecclesiastical formalities for the convalidation of marriage.[20] According to this doctrine the *"ab acatholicis nati"* of canon 1099, § 2, would be released from the formalities of convalidation as determined in canons 1133-1137, and a marriage attempted by them which was invalid because of some diriment impediment or lack of consent would be convalidated by the cessation of that impediment or the giving of consent without any formalities whatsoever, as long as that consent were present which is required by the natural law.

2°. In utroque casu, si praesto sit alius sacerdos qui adesse possit, vocari et, una cum testibus, matrimonio assistere debet, salva coniugii validitate coram solis testibus.

[17] Dillon, *Common Law Marriage,* The Catholic University of America Canon Law Studies, n. 153 (Washington, D. C.: The Catholic University of America Press, 1942), p. 59.

[18] Canons 1133-1137.

[19] Canon 1133, § 2.

[20] Cappello, "Utrum acatholici exempti a forma celebrationis matrimonii subsint, necne, normis praefinitis in can. 1133 seq. ad simplicem convalidationem quod attinet"—*Jus Pontificium,* XX (1940), 25-27.

It is readily granted that the form of marriage will never be required of the persons considered in canon 1099, § 2. Provided all the conditions of the canon are fulfilled, therefore, such persons are not bound to observe the form of marriage prescribed by law even when such a renewal of consent according to the prescribed form is required for the convalidation of a marriage according to the norms of canons 1133-1137. If one will limit the doctrine of Cappello to this one case, it is certainly sound teaching.

To maintain, however, that those persons born of non-Catholics as mentioned in canon 1099, § 2, are released from any renewal consent whatsoever, even in cases when required renewal of consent need not be made according to the form required in canon 1094, is to propose a teaching that is not easily sustained in the law itself and one that is defended only by Cappello.

It is, first of all, arbitrary to say that the formalities of convalidation are reducible to the form of marriage. It seems preferable to admit that the requirement of the renewal of consent is a distinct notion from that of the obligation to observe the form of marriage, and that Catholics and baptized non-Catholics alike are bound to renew matrimonial consent when there is question of the simple convalidation of marriage.[21] This renewal of consent is required by ecclesiastical law for validity.[22] There can be found no exemption in the law from this renewal of consent allowable to those persons who are released from the obligation of observing the canonical form of marriage. It seems, therefore, that even such persons are held to the renewal of consent when there is question of the simple convalidation of marriage.

As regards the *"ab acatholicis nati"* of canon 1099, § 2, it is safe to conclude that though they are bound to renew matrimonial consent when there is question of the convalidation of marriage, they are not bound to renew their consent according to the prescribed form of marriage. All the other provisions of canons 1133-1137 remain in force, however, even in the case of such persons.

[21] Ayrinhac-Lydon, *Marriage Legislation in the New Code of Canon Law,* n. 308.

[22] Canon 1133, § 2.

CONCLUSIONS

1. The notion of apostate parents in relation to canon 1099, § 2, includes not only those persons who have defected from the Christian faith, but also those who have defected from the Catholic faith.

2. If at the time of a child's birth both of its parents are Catholics, it can never claim the exemption of canon 1099, § 2, as the law now stands.

3. An illegitimate child is considered born of non-Catholics if either of its natural parents is a non-Catholic at the time of its birth.

4. The religious education of the *"ab acatholicis nati"* in reference to their exemption from the Catholic form of marriage must be considered as that which was given before the age of seven completed years onward, even in the case of those who do not reach the use of reason before the age of seven completed years but especially with reference to those who do.

5. The voluntary reception of a sacrament after Catholic baptism demonstrates conclusively that the individual considered in canon 1099, § 2, has been reared a Catholic sufficiently to induce his obligation to the canonical form of marriage. This is true even in the case of those who have received the sacrament before they had completed the seventh year of their life, provided that they possessed the use of reason when the sacrament was received.

6. A tacit acceptance of the faith suffices to induce the obligation to the canonical form of marriage for the *"ab acatholicis nati"* who have received a Catholic baptism.

7. The *"ab acatholicis nati"* of canon 1099, § 2, are released from the extraordinary form of canon 1098.

8. Marriages contracted between the *"ab acatholicis nati"* and Orientals who are not bound to any form for the contracting of marriage are valid even if the canonical from has not been observed.

9. It is the more probable opinion that the inter-marriage of persons considered in canon 1099, § 2, is valid even though they did not observe the canonical form of marriage.

BIBLIOGRAPHY

SOURCES

Acta Apostolicae Sedis, Commentarium Officiale, Romae (Civitate Vaticana), 1909—

Acta Sanctae Sedis, 41 vols., Romae, 1865-1908.

Bouscaren, T. L., *The Canon Law Digest*, 2 vols., Milwaukee: The Bruce Publishing Company, 1934-1943.

Canones et Decreta Sacrosancti Oecumenici Concilii Tridenti sub Paulo III, Julio III, et Pio IV Pontificibus Maximis, Editio Stereotypa, Ratisbonae, 1903.

Codex Iuris Canonici Pii X Pontificis Maximi iussu digestus Benedicti XV auctoritate promulgatus, Romae: Typis Polyglottis Vaticanis, 1917. Reimpressio, 1919.

Codicis Iuris Canonici Fontes cura Emi Petri Card. Gasparri editi, 9 vols., Romae: Typis Polyglottis Vaticania, 1923-1939. (Vols. VII, VIII, IX, ed. cura et studio Emi Iustiniani Serédi.)

Collectanea S. Congregationis de Propaganda Fide, 2 vols., Romae: Typographia Polyglotta S. C. de Propaganda Fide, 1907.

Concilii Tridentini Diariorum, Actorum, Epistularum, Tractatuum, Nova Collectio, ed. Societas Goerresiana, 13 vols., Friburgi Brisgoviae: Herder, 1901-1938; Vol. IX, ed. S. Ehses, 1924.

Decretales D. Gregorii Papae IX, una cum Glossis Restitutae, Romae, 1582.

Decretum Gratiani emendatum et notationibus illustratum una cum glossis Gregorii XIII, Pont. Max., iussu editum, 2 vols., Romae, 1582.

Jaffé, Phillipus, *Regesta Pontificium Romanorum ab condita Ecclesia ad annum post Christum natum MCXCVIII*, 2. ed., correctam et auctam auspiciis Gulielmi Wattenbach curaverunt F. Kaltenbrunner (ad annum 590), P. Ewald (590-882), S. Loewenfeld (882-1198), 2 vols., in 1, Lipsiae, 1885-1888.

Le Plat, J., *Canones et Decreta Sacrosancti Oecumenici et Generalis Concilii Tridentini*, Antwerpiae: Plantin, 1779.

Mansi, Ioannes, *Sacrorum Conciliorum Nova et Amplissima Collectio*, 53 vols. in 60, Parisiis, 1901-1927.

Sacrae Romanae Rotae Decisions seu Sententiae quae prodierunt ab anno 1909, Romae: Typis Polyglottis Vaticanis, 1912—

Schroeder, J., *Canons and Decrees of the Council of Trent*, St. Louis: Herder Book Co., 1941.

Theiner, Augustin, *Acta Genuina SS. Oecumenici Concilii Tridentini*, 2 vols., Zagabriae, Croatia, 1874.

Waterworth, J., *The Canons and Decrees of the Sacred and Oecumical Council of Trent*, London: C. Dolman, 1848.

REFERENCE WORKS

Augustine, Charles, *A Commentary on the New Code of Canon Law*, 8 vols., Vol. V, St. Louis: B. Herder, 1919; Vol. V, 5. revised ed., St. Louis: B. Herder, 1935.

Ayrinhac, H. A., *Marriage Legislation in the New Code of Canon Law*, 2. revised edition by P. J. Lydon, New York, Boston, Cincinnati, Chicago, San Francisco: Benziger Brothers, Inc., 1938.

Aertnys, J.-Damen, C. A., *Theologia Moralis*, 11. ed., 2 vols., Taurini-Romae: Marietti, 1928.

Bareille, G., *Code du Droit Canonique*, 2. ed., Paris: Cordeilhac-Soubiron, 1925.

Bargilliat, M., *Praelectiones Juris Canonici*, 37. ed., 2 vols., Parisiis: apud Baston, Berche et Pagis, 1923.

Benedictus XIV, *De Synodo Dioecesana*, 2 vols., Romae, 1767.

Beste, Udalricus, *Introductio in Codicem*, editio altera, Collegeville, Minn.: St. John's Abbey Press, 1944.

Brennan, J. H., *The Simple Convalidation of Marriage*, The Catholic University of America Canon Law Studies, n. 102, Washington, D. C.: The Catholic University of America, 1937.

Cance, Adrien, *Le Code de Droit Canonique*, 16. ed., 3 vols., Paris: J. Cabalda et Fils, 1930.

Cappello, Felix M., *Tractatus Canonico-Moralis de Sacramentis*, Vol. III, *De Matrimonio*, Taurini: Marietti, 1923; Vol. III, 4. ed., Romae: apud Aedes Universitatis Gregorianae, 1939.

Carberry, J. J., *The Juridical Form of Marriage*, The Catholic University of America Canon Law Studies, n. 84, Washington, D. C.: The Catholic University of America, 1934.

Cerato, P., *Matrimonium a Codice Iuris Canonici Integre Desumptum*, 4. ed., Patavii: Typis Seminarii: 1929.

Chelodi, Ioannes, *Ius Matrimoniale*, 4. ed., a V. Dalpiaz, Tridenti: Libreria Moderna Editrice A. Ardesi, 1937.

Cicognani, A. G., *Commentarium ad Librum I Codicis*, Romae: ex Schola Typographia "Piis X," 1925.

———, *Canon Law*, authorized English version by O'Hara and Brennan, 2. revised ed., Philadelphia: Dolphin Press, 1935.

Claeys Bouuaert, F.-Simeon, G., *Manuale Juris Canonici*, 3 vols., Gandae et Leodii: Dessain; Vols. I and III, 3. ed., 1930; Vol. II, 1931.

Coronata, Matthaeus Conte a, *Institutiones Iuris Canonici*, 5 vols., Taurini: Marietti, 1928-1936; Vol. IV, *De Delictis et Poenis*, 1935.

De Smet, A., *Tractatus Theologico-Canonicus de Sponsalibus et Matrimonio*, 4. ed., Brugis: Car. Beyaert, 1927.

Dillon, R. E., *Common Law Marriage*, the Catholic University of America Canon Law Studies, n. 153, Washington, D. C.: The Catholic University of America Press, 1942.

Doheny, William J., *Canonical Procedure in Matrimonial Cases*, Milwaukee: Bruce Publishing Co., 1938.

Farrugia, Nicolaus, *De Matrimonio et Causis Matrimonialibus-Tractatus Canonico-Moralis iuxta Codicem Juris Canonici*, Taurini-Romae: Typis Polyglottis Vaticanis, 1924.

Gasparri, P., *Tractatus Canonicus de Matrimonio*, editio nova ad mentem *Codicis Iuris Canonici*, 2 vols., Romae: Typis Polyglottis Vaticanis, 1932.

Goodwine, J. G., *The Reception of Converts*, The Catholic University of America Canon Law Studies, n. 198, Washington, D. C.: The Catholic University of America Press, 1944.

Gougnard, A., *Tractatus de Matrimonio*, 7. ed., Mechliniae: Dessain, 1931.

Jone, H., *Gesetzbuch des kanonischen Rechtes*, 3 vols., Paderborn: Ferdinand Schöningh, 1939-1941.

Knecht, A., *Handbuch des katholischen Eherechts*, Freiburg: B. Herder, 1928.

Leitner, Martin, *Handbuch des katholischen Eherechts*, 3. ed., Paderborn: Ferdinand Schöningh, 1920.

Maroto, Phillipus, *Institutiones Iuris Canonici ad Normam Novi Codicis*, 2 vols., Vol. I, 3. ed., Romae: apud Commentarium pro Religiosis, 1921.

Marx, Adolph, *The Declaration of Nullity of Marriages Contracted Outside the Church*, The Catholic University of America Canon Law Studies, n. 182, Washington, D. C.: The Catsolic University of America Press, 1943.

Michiels, Gommarus, *Principia Generalia de Personis in Ecclesia*, Lublin: Braaschaat, 1932.

Nau, L. J., *Manual on the Marriage Laws of the Code of Canon Law*, 2. ed., New York and Cincinnati: Frederick Pustet Co., Inc., 1934.

Noldin, H.-Schmitt, A., *Summa Theologiae Moralis*, 24. ed., 4 vols. in 3, Oeniponte: Typis et Sumptibus F. Rauch, 1936.

Pallavicino, Cardinalis Pietro Sforza, *Historia Concilii Tridentini*, translated by J. B. Giattino, 3 vols., Antwerpiae, 1670.

Payen, G., *De Matrimonio in Missionibus ac potissimum in Sinis, Tractatus Practicus et Casus*, editio altera, 3 vols., Zi-ka-wei: In Typographia T'ou-sè-wè, 1935-1936.

Perisse Frères, Libraire Editeur, *Histoire du Concile de Trente*, 2 vols., Paris, 1851.

Petrovits, J. J., *The New Church Law on Matrimony*, 2. ed., Philadelphia: John Joseph McVey, 1926.

Prümmer, Dominicus M., *Manuale Theologiae Moralis*, 8. ed., ed. E. Münch, 3 vols., Friburgi Brisgoviae: B. Herder & Co., 1935-1936.

Raus, J. B., *Institutiones Canonicae*, 2. ed., Londini-Parisiis: Emmanuel Vitte, 1931.

Rossi, Jos., *De Matrimonii Celebratione iuxta, C. I. C.*, Romae: Pustet, 1924.

Sarpi, P., *Histoire du Concile de Trente*, translated into French by Francis le Courayer, 2 vols., Basle: J. Brandmüller et Fils, 1738.

Schenk, Francis J., *The Matrimonial Impediments of Mixed Religion and Disparity of Cult,* The Catholic University of America Canon Law Studies, n. 51, Washington D. C.: The Catholic University of America, 1929.

Sipos, Stephanus, *Enchiridion Juris Canonici,* 3. ed., Pécs: "Haladás R. T.," 1936.

Thomas Aquinas, St., *Summa Theologica,* 6 vols., Taurini: Marietti, 1932.

Triebs, F., *Praktisches Handbuch des geltenden kanonischen Eherechts in Vergleichung mit dem deutschen staatlichen Eherecht,* Teil I-IV in einem Band, Gesamtausgabe, Breslau: Ostdeutsche Verlagsanstalt, 1933.

Vermeersch, A.-Creusen, J., *Epitome Iuris Canonici,* 2. ed., 3 vols., Mechliniae: H. Dessain, 1925; Vol. II, 5. ed., 1934; Vol. III, 5. ed., 1936.

Vlaming, T., *Praelectiones Iuris Matrimonii,* 3. ed., 2 vols., Bussum in Hollandia: Brand, Vol. I, 1919; Vol. II, 1921.

Vromant, G., *Ius Missionariorum,* Vol. V, *De Matrimonio,* Louvain: Museum Lessianum, 1931.

Wernz, F. X., *Ius Decretalium,* 6 vols., Romae, 1898-1905.

——— - Vidal, P., *Ius Canonicum,* 7 vols. in 8, Romae: apud Aedes Universitatis Gregorianae, 1923-1938; Vol. V, 2. ed., 1928.

Periodicals

American Ecclesiastical Review, The (formerly *The Ecclesiastical Review*), Philadelphia, 1889-1943; Baltimore, 1944—

Ami du Clergé, L', Paris, Langres, 1878—

Apollinaris, Romae, 1928—

Clergy Review, The, London, 1931—

Homilectic and Pastoral Review, The, New York, 1900—

Irish Theological Quarterly, The, Dublin, 1906—

Jurist, The, Washington, D. C., 1941—

Jus Pontificium, Romae, 1921—

Nouvelle Revue Théologique, Paris, 1869—

Periodica de Re Canonica et Morali utili praesertim Religiosis et Missionariis, Brugis, 1905-1927.

——— *de Re Morali, Canonica, Liturgica,* Brugis, 1928-1936; Romae, 1937—

Theologische-praktische Quartalschrift, Linz, 1852—

Articles

Allen, W. F., "The Test of Catholicity under Canon 1099,"—*The Jurist,* III (1943), 595-602.

———, "The Test of Catholicity under Canon 1099: Objections Resolved,"—*The Jurist,* IV (1944), 124-129.

Beijersbergen, H., "Casus"—*Periodica,* XXX (1941), 46-51.

Cappello, F. M., "Quinam censeantur 'ab acatholicis nati' ad normam can. 1099, § 2, ideoque a canonica forma celebrationis matrimonii immunes"—*Periodica,* XX (1931), 77-81.

———, "Utrum acatholici exempti a forma celebrationis matrimonii subsint, necne, normis praefinitis in can. 1133 seq. ad simplicem convalidationem quo attinet"—*Jus Pontificium,* XX (1940), 25-27.

Dalpiaz, Vigilius, "An a catholicis nati et catholice baptizati, sed ab infantili aetate acatholice educati, praescripta matrimonii forma teneantur"—*Apollinaris,* X (1937), 105-107.

Graneris, Jos., "De iis qui sine ulla religione adoleverunt"—*Apollinaris,* XI (1938), 568-571.

Jone, H., "Die Verpflictung der Form bei der Eheschliessung"—*Theologisch-praktische Quartalschrift,* LXXX (1927), 556-559.

———, "Die Verpflictung der Form bei der Eheschliessung"—*Theologisch-praktische Quartalschrift,* LXXXII (1929), 780-783.

Hannan, Jerome, "Validity of Marriage. Canons 1099, and 1070"—*The Ecclesiastical Review,* CIX (1943), 453-456.

Maroto, P., "De vi verborum can. 1099, § 2, 'ab acatholicis nati' "—*Apollinaris,* III (1930), 601-616.

Mahoney, E. J., " 'Ab Acatholicis Nati' (can. 1099, § 2)"—*The Clergy Review,* XVI (1939), 511-520.

McCloskey, J. A., "Post-Code Opinions on the Obligation of Heretics to Observe Ecclesiastical Laws"—*The Jurist,* III (1943), 480-492.

Oesterle, G., "Form der Eheschliessung für die 'nati ab acatholicis,' canon 1099, § 2"—*Theologisch-Praktische Quartalschrift,* LXXXV (1932), 352-361.

O'Donnell, M. J., "*Ne temere* and the New Code"—*The Irish Theological Quarterly,* XV (1919), 140-155.

Schaaf, V., "An Exemption from the Canonical Form of Marriage"—*The Ecclesiastical Review,* LXXXIII (1930), 484-496.

———, "Are children born of Catholics exempt from canonical form of marriage?"—*The Ecclesiastical Review* XCIV (1936), 630-633.

———, "Exemption of *'ab acatholicis nati'* under the decree *'Ne temere'* "—*The Ecclesiastical Review,* XCIX (1936), 188-189.

———, "Exemption from the Canonical form of Marriage and from disparity of Cult"—*The Ecclesiastical Review,* LXXXVI (1932), 79-82.

ABBREVIATIONS

AAS—Acta Apostolicae Sedis.
ASS—Acta Sanctae Sedis.
Coll. S. C. P. F.—Collectanea S. C. de Propaganda Fide.
Fontes—Codicis Iuris Canonici Fontes.
S. C. C.—Sacra Congregatio Concilii.
S. C. P. F.—Sacra Congregatio de Propaganda Fide.
S. C. S. Off.—Sacra Congregatio Sancti Officii.
S. C. S. Off.—Suprema Congregatio Sancti Officii.
S. R. R.—Sacra Romana Rota.

ALPHABETICAL INDEX

BIOGRAPHICAL NOTE

Warren Louis Boudreaux was born January 25, 1918, in Berwick, Louisiana. After completing his primary education in the Berwick Junior High School, he entered St. Joseph's Preparatory Seminary, St. Benedict, Louisiana, graduating in June, 1936. In the fall of that year he entered Notre Dame Seminary, New Orleans, Louisiana, where he completed his course in Philosophy in 1938. He made the first year of his Theological Studies at the Grand Séminaire de S. Sulpice, Paris, France. At the outbreak of the war in Europe he returned to the United States and finished his Theological Studies at Notre Dame Seminary. He was ordained to the Sacred Priesthood on May 30, 1942. Following a year of parochial work in St. Michael's Parish, Crowley, Louisiana, he enrolled in the School of Canon Law at the Catholic University of America in September, 1943. In May, 1944, he received the degree of the Baccalaureate in Canon Law, and in May, 1945, the degree of the Licentiate in Canon Law.

CANON LAW STUDIES *

1. Freriks, Rev. Celestine A., C.PP.S., J.C.D., Religious Congregations in Their External Relations, 121 pp., 1916.
2. Galliher, Rev. Daniel M., O.P., J.C.D., Canonical Elections, 117 pp., 1917.
3. Borkowski, Rev. Aurelius L., O.F.M., J.C.D., De Confraternitatibus Ecclesiasticis, 136 pp., 1918.
4. Castillo, Rev. Cayo, J.C.D., Disertacion Historico-Canonica sobre la Potestad del Cabildo en Sede Vacante o Impedida del Vicario Capitular, 99 pp., 1919 (1918).
5. Kubelbeck, Rev. William J., S.T.B., J.C.D., The Sacred Penitentiaria and Its Relation to Faculties of Ordinaries and Priests, 129 pp., 1918.
6. Petrovits, Rev. Joseph, J.C., S.T.D., J.C.D., The New Church Law on Matrimony, X-461 pp., 1919.
7. Hickey, Rev. John J., S.T.B., J.C.D., Irregularities and Simple Impediments in the New Code of Canon Law, 100 pp., 1920.
8. Klekotka, Rev. Peter J., S.T.B., J.C.D., Diocesan Consultors, 179 pp., 1920.
9. Wanenmacher, Rev. Francis, J.C.D., The Evidence in Ecclesiastical Procedure Affecting the Marriage Bond, 1920 (Printed 1935).
10. Golden, Rev. Henry Francis, J.C.D., Parochial Benefices in the New Code, IV-119 pp., 1921 (Printed 1925).
11. Koudelka, Rev. Charles J., J.C.D., Pastors, Their Rights and Duties According to the New Code of Canon Law, 211 pp., 1921.
12. Melo, Rev. Antonius, O.F.M., J.C.D., De Exemptione Regularium, X-188 pp., 1921.
13. Schaaf, Rev. Valentine Theodore, O.F.M., S.T.B., J.C.D., The Cloister, X-180 pp., 1921.
14. Burke, Rev. Thomas Joseph, S.T.D., J.C.D., Competence in Ecclesiastical Tribunals, IV-117 pp., 1922.
15. Leech, Rev. George Leo, J.C.D., A Comparative Study of the Constitution "Apostolicae Sedis" and the "Codex Juris Canonici," 179 pp., 1922.
16. Motry, Rev. Hubert Louis, S.T.D., J.C.D., Diocesan Faculties According to the Code of Canon Law, II-167 pp., 1922.
17. Murphy, Rev. George Lawrence, J.C.D., Delinquencies and Penalties in the Administration and the Reception of the Sacraments, IV-121 pp., 1923.
18. O'Reilly, Rev. John Anthony, S.T.B., J.C.D., Ecclesiastical Sepulture in the New Code of Canon Law, II-129 pp., 1923.

---

* From nn. 1-100 inclusive only nn. 25 and 57 are still obtainable.

From n. 101 onward all numbers are available except the following: nn. 101-118 inclusive, and also n. 122.

19. MICHALICKA, REV. WENCESLAS CYRILL, O.S.B., J.C.D., Judicial Procedure in Dismissal of Clerical Exempt Religious, 107 pp., 1923.
20. DARGIN, REV. EDWARD VINCENT, S.T.B., J.C.D., Reserved Cases According to the Code of Canon Law, IV-103 pp., 1924.
21. GODFREY, REV. JOHN A., S.T.B., J.C.D., The Right of Patronage According to the Code of Canon Law, 153 pp., 1924.
22. HAGEDORN, REV. FRANCIS EDWARD, J.C.D., General Legislation on Indulgences, II-154 pp., 1924.
23. KING, REV. JAMES IGNATIUS, J.C.D., The Administration of the Sacraments to Dying Non-Catholics, V-141 pp., 1924.
24. WINSLOW, REV. FRANCIS JOSEPH, O.F.M., J.C.D., Vicars and Prefects Apostolic, IV-149 pp., 1924.
25. CORREA, REV. JOSE SERVELION, S.T.L., J.C.D., La Potestad Legislativa de la Iglesia Catolica, IV-127 pp., 1925.
26. DUGAN, REV. HENRY FRANCIS, A.M., J.C.D., The Judiciary Department of the Diocesan Curia, 87 pp., 1925.
27. KELLER, REV. CHARLES FREDERICK, S.T.B., J.C.D., Mass Stipends, 167 pp., 1925.
28. PASCHANG, REV. JOHN LINUS, J.C.D., The Sacramentals According to the Code of Canon Law, 129 pp., 1925.
29. PIONTEK, REV. CYRILLUS, O.F.M., S.T.B., J.C.D., De Indulto Exclaustrationis necnon Saecularizationis, XIII-289 pp., 1925.
30. KEARNEY, REV. RICHARD JOSEPH, S.T.B., J.C.D., Sponsors at Baptism According to the Code of Canon Law, IV-127 pp., 1925.
31. BARTLETT, REV. CHESTER JOSEPH, A.M., LL.B., J.C.D., The Tenure of Parochial Property in the United States of America, V-108 pp., 1926.
32. KILKER, REV. ADRIAN JEROME, J.C.D., Extreme Unction, V-425 pp., 1926.
33. MCCORMICK, REV. ROBERT EMMETT, J.C.D., Confessors of Religious, VIII-266 pp., 1926.
34. MILLER, REV. NEWTON THOMAS, J.C.D., Founded Masses According to the Code of Canon Law, VII-93 pp., 1926.
35. ROELKER, REV. EDWARD G., S.T.D., J.C.D., Principles of Privilege According to the Code of Canon Law, XI-166 pp., 1926.
36. BAKALARCZYK, REV. RICHARDUS, M.I.C., J.U.D., De Novitiatu, VIII-208 pp., 1927.
37. PIZZUTI, REV. LAWRENCE, O.F.M., J.U.L., De Parochis Religiosis, 1927. (Not Printed.)
38. BLILEY, REV. NICHOLAS MARTIN, O.S.B., J.C.D., Altars According to the Code of Canon Law, XIX-132 pp., 1927.
39. BROWN, MR. BRENDAN FRANCIS, A.B., LL.M., J.U.D., The Canonical Juristic Personality with Special Reference to its Status in the United States of America, V-212 pp., 1927.
40. CAVANAUGH, REV. WILLIAM THOMAS, C.P., J.U.D., The Reservation of the Blessed Sacrament, VIII-101 pp., 1927.

41. DOHENY, REV. WILLIAM J., C.S.C., A.B., J.U.D., Church Property: Modes of Acquisition, X-118 pp., 1927.
42. FELDHAUS, REV. ALOYSIUS H., C.PP.S., J.C.D., Oratories, IX-141 pp., 1927.
43. KELLY, REV. JAMES PATRICK, A.B., J.C.D., The Jurisdiction of the Simple Confessor, X-208 pp., 1927.
44. NEUBERGER, REV. NICHOLAS J., J.C.D., Canon 6 or the Relation of the Codex Juris Canonici to the Preceding Legislation, V-95 pp., 1927.
45. O'KEEFE, REV. GERALD MICHAEL, J.C.D., Matrimonial Dispensations, Powers of Bishops, Priests, and Confessors, VIII-232 pp., 1927.
46. QUIGLEY, REV. JOSEPH A. M., A.B., J.C.D., Condemned Societies, 139 pp., 1927.
47. ZAPLOTNIK, REV. JOHANNES LEO, J.C.D., De Vicariis Foraneis, X-142 pp., 1927.
48. DUSKIE, REV. JOHN ALOYSIUS, A.B., J.C.D., The Canonical Status of the Orientals in the United States, VIII-196 pp., 1928.
49. HYLAND, REV. FRANCIS EDWARD, J.C.D., Excommunication, Its Nature, Historical Development and Effects, VIII-181 pp., 1928.
50. REINMANN, REV. GERALD JOSEPH, O.M.C., J.C.D., The Third Order Secular of Saint Francis, 201 pp., 1928.
51. SCHENK, REV. FRANCIS J., J.C.D., The Matrimonial Impediments of Mixed Religion and Disparity of Cult, XVI-318 pp., 1929.
52. COADY, REV. JOHN JOSEPH, S.T.D., J.U.D., A.M., The Appointment of Pastors, VIII-150 pp., 1929.
53. KAY, REV. THOMAS HENRY, J.C.D., Competence in Matrimonial Procedure, VIII-164 pp., 1929.
54. TURNER, REV. SIDNEY JOSEPH, C.P., J.U.D., The Vow of Poverty, XLIX-217 pp., 1929.
55. KEARNEY, REV. RAYMOND A., A.B., S.T.D., J.C.D., The Principles of Delegation, VII-149 pp., 1929.
56. CONRAN, REV. EDWARD JAMES, A.B., J.C.D., The Interdict, V-163 pp., 1930.
57. O'NEILL, REV. WILLIAM H., J.C.D., Papal Rescripts of Favor, VII-218 pp., 1930.
58. BASTNAGEL, REV. CLEMENT VINCENT, J.U.D., The Appointment of Parochial Adjutants and Assistants, XV-257 pp., 1930.
59. FERRY, REV. WILLIAM A., A.B., J.C.D., Stole Fees, V-136 pp., 1930.
60. COSTELLO, REV. JOHN MICHAEL, A.B., J.C.D., Domicile and Quasi-Domicile, VII-201 pp., 1930.
61. KREMER, REV. MICHAEL NICHOLAS, A.B., S.T.B., J.C.D., Church Support in the United States, VI-136 pp., 1930.
62. ANGULO, REV. LUIS, C.M., J.C.D., Legislation de la Iglesia sobre la intencion en la application de la Santa Misa, VII-104 pp., 1931.
63. FREY, REV. WOLFGANG NORBERT, O.S.B., A.B., J.C.D., The Act of Religious Profession, VIII-174 pp., 1931.

64. Roberts, Rev. James Brendan, A.B., J.C.D., The Banns of Marriage, XIV-140 pp., 1931.
65. Ryder, Rev. Raymond Aloysius, A.B., J.C.D., Simony, IX-151 pp., 1931.
66. Campagna, Rev. Angelo, Ph.D., J.U.D., Il Vicario Generale del Vescovo, VII-205 pp., 1931.
67. Cox, Rev. Joseph Godfrey, A.B., J.C.D., The Administration of Seminaries, VI-124 pp., 1931.
68. Gregory, Rev. Donald J., J.U.D., The Pauline Privilege, XV-165 pp., 1931.
69. Donohue, Rev. John F., J.C.D., The Impediment of Crime, VII-110 pp., 1931.
70. Dooley, Rev. Eugene A., O.M.I., J.C.D., Church Law on Sacred Relics, IX-143 pp., 1931.
71. Orth, Rev. Clement Raymond, O.M.C., J.C.D., The Approbation of Religious Institutes, 171 pp., 1931.
72. Pernicone, Rev. Joseph M., A.B., J.C.D., The Ecclesiastical Prohibition of Books, XII-267 pp., 1932.
73. Clinton, Rev. Connell, A.B., J.C.D., The Paschal Precept, IX-108 pp., 1932.
74. Donnelly, Rev. Francis B., A.M., S.T.L., J.C.D., The Diocesan Synod, VIII-125 pp., 1932.
75. Torrente, Rev. Camilo, C.M.F., J.C.D., Las Procesiones Sagradas, V-145 pp., 1932.
76. Murphy, Rev. Edwin J., C.PP.S., J.C.D., Suspension Ex Informata Conscientia, XI-122 pp., 1932.
77. MacKenzie, Rev. Eric F., A.M., S.T.L., J.C.D., The Delict of Heresy in its Commission, Penalization, Absolution, VII-124 pp., 1932.
78. Lyons, Rev. Avitus E., S.T.B., J.C.D., The Collegiate Tribunal of First Instance, XI-147 pp., 1932.
79. Connolly, Rev. Thomas A., J.C.D., Appeals, XI-195, pp., 1932.
80. Sangmeister, Rev. Joseph V., A.B., J.C.D., Force and Fear as Precluding Matrimonial Consent, V-211 pp., 1932.
81. Jaeger, Rev. Leo A., A.B., J.C.D., The Administration of Vacant and Quasi-Vacant Episcopal Sees in the United States, IX-229 pp., 1932.
32. Rimlinger, Rev. Herbert T., J.C.D., Error Invalidating Matrimonial Consent, VII-79 pp., 1932.
83. Barrett, Rev. John D. M., S.S., J.C.D., A Comparative Study of the Third Plenary Council of Baltimore and the Code, IX-221 pp., 1932.
84. Carberry, Rev. John J., Ph.D., S.T.D., J.C.D., The Juridical Form of Marriage, X-177 pp., 1934.
85. Dolan, Rev. John L., A.B., J.C.D., The Defensor Vinculi, XII-157 pp., 1934.
86. Hannan, Rev. Jerome D., A.M., S.T.D., LL.B., J.C.D., The Canon Law of Wills, IX-517 pp., 1934.

87. LEMIEUX, REV. DELISE A., A.M., J.C.D., The Sentence in Ecclesiastical Procedure, IX-131 pp., 1934.
88. O'ROURKE, REV. JAMES J., A.B., J.C.D., Parish Registers, VII-109 pp., 1934.
89. TIMLIN, REV. BARTHOLOMEW, O.F.M., A.M., J.C.D., Conditional Matrimonial Consent, X-381 pp., 1934.
90. WAHL, REV. FRANCIS X., A.B., J.C.D., The Matrimonial Impediments of Consanguinity and Affinity, VI-125 pp., 1934.
91. WHITE, REV. ROBERT J., A.B., LL.B., S.T.B., J.C.D., Canonical Ante-Nuptial Promises and the Civil Law, VI-152 pp., 1934.
92. HERRERA, REV. ANTONIO PARRA, O.C.D., J.C.D., Legislacion Ecclesiastica sobra el Ayuno y la Abstinencia, XI-191 pp., 1935.
93. KENNEDY, REV. EDWIN J., J.C.D., The Special Matrimonial Process in Cases of Evident Nullity, X-165 pp., 1935.
94. MANNING, REV. JOHN J., A.B., J.C.D., Presumption of Law in Matrimonial Procedure, XI-111 pp., 1935.
95. MOEDER, REV. JOHN M., J.C.D., The Proper Bishop for Ordination and Dismissorial Letters, VII-135 pp., 1935.
96. O'MARA, REV. WILLIAM A., A.B., J.C.D., Canonical Causes for Matrimonial Dispensations, IX-155 pp., 1935.
97. REILLY, REV. PETER, J.C.D., Residence of Pastors, IX-81 pp., 1935.
98. SMITH, REV. MARINER T., O.P., S.T.Lr., J.C.D., The Penal Law for Religious, VIII-169 pp., 1935.
99. WHALEN, REV. DONALD W., A.M., J.C.D., The Value of Testimonial Evidence in Matrimonial Procedure, XIII-297 pp., 1935.
100. CLEARY, REV. JOSEPH F., J.C.D., Canonical Limitations on the Alienation of Church Property, VIII-141 pp., 1936.
101. GLYNN, REV. JOHN C., J.C.D., The Promoter of Justice, XX-337 pp., 1936.
102. BRENNAN, REV. JAMES H., S.S., M.A., S.T.B., J.C.D., The Simple Convalidation of Marriage, VI-135 pp., 1937.
103. BRUNINI, REV. JOSEPH BERNARD, J.C.D., The Clerical Obligations of Canons 139 and 142, X-121 pp., 1937.
104. CONNOR, REV. MAURICE, A.B., J.C.D., The Administrative Removal of Pastors, VIII-159 pp., 1937.
105. GUILFOYLE, REV. MERLIN JOSEPH, J.C.D., Custom, XI-144 pp., 1937.
106. HUGHES, REV. JAMES AUSTIN, A.B., A.M., J.C.D., Witnesses in Criminal Trials of Clerics, IX-140 pp., 1937.
107. JANSEN, REV. RAYMOND J., A.B., S.T.L., J.C.D., Canonical Provisions for Catechetical Instruction, VII-153 pp., 1937.
108. KEALY, REV. JOHN JAMES, A.B., J.C.D., The Introductory Libellus in Church Court Procedure, XI-121 pp., 1937.
109. McMANUS, REV. JAMES EDWARD, C.SS.R., J.C.D., The Administration of Temporal Goods in Religious Institutes, XVI-196 pp., 1937.

110. MORIARTY, REV. EUGENE JAMES, J.C.D., Oaths in Ecclesiastical Courts, X-115 pp., 1937.
111. RAINER, REV. ELIGIUS GEORGE, C.SS.R., J.C.D., Suspension of Clerics, XVII-249 pp., 1937.
112. REILLY, REV. THOMAS F., C.SS.R., J.C.D., Visitation of Religious, VI-195 pp., 1938.
113. MORIARTY, REV. FRANCIS E., C.SS.R., J.C.D., The Extraordinary Absolution from Censures, XV-334 pp., 1938.
114. CONNOLLY, REV. NICHOLAS P., J.C.D., The Canonical Erection of Parishes, X-132 pp., 1938.
115. DONOVAN, REV. JAMES JOSEPH, J.C.D., The Pastor's Obligation in Prenuptial Investigation, XII-322 pp., 1938.
116. HARRIGAN, REV. ROBERT J., M.A., S.T.B., J.C.D., The Radical Sanation of Invalid Marriages, VIII-208 pp., 1938.
117. BOFFA, REV. CONRAD HUMBERT, J.C.D., Canonical Provisions for Catholic Schools, VII-211 pp., 1939.
118. PARSONS, REV. ANSCAR JOHN, O.M.Cap., J.C.D., Canonical Elections, XII-236 pp., 1939.
119. REILLY, REV. EDWARD MICHAEL, A.B., J.C.D., The General Norms of Dispensation, XII-156 pp., 1939.
120. RYAN, REV. GERALD ALOYSIUS, A.B., J.C.D., Principles of Episcopal Jurisdiction, XII-172 pp., 1939.
121. BURTON, REV. FRANCIS JAMES, C.S.C., A.B., J.C.D., A Commentary on Canon 1125, X-222 pp., 1940.
122. MIASKIEWICZ, REV. FRANCIS SIGISMUND, J.C.D., Supplied Jurisdiction According to Canon 209, XII-340 pp., 1940.
123. RICE, REV. PATRICK WILLIAM, A.B., J.C.D., Proof of Death in Prenuptial Investigation, VIII-156 pp., 1940.
124. ANGLIN, REV. THOMAS FRANCIS, M.S., J.C.D., The Eucharistic Fast, VIII-183 pp., 1941.
125. COLEMAN, REV. JOHN JEROME, J.C.D., The Minister of Confirmation, VI-153 pp., 1941.
126. DOWNS, REV. JOHN EMMANUEL, A.B., J.C.D., The Concept of Clerical Immunity, XI-163 pp., 1941.
127. ESSWEIN, REV. ANTHONY ALBERT, J.C.D., Extrajudicial Penal Powers of Ecclesiastical Superiors, X-144 pp., 1941.
128. FARRELL, REV. BENJAMIN FRANCIS, M.A., S.T.L., J.C.D., The Rights and Duties of the Local Ordinary Regarding Congregations of Women Religious of Pontifical Approval, V-195 pp., 1941.
129. FEENEY, REV. THOMAS JOHN, A.B., S.T.L., J.C.D., Restitutio in Integrum, VI-169 pp., 1941.
130. FINDLAY, REV. STEPHEN WILLIAM, O.S.B., A.B., J.C.D., Canonical Norms Governing the Deposition and Degradation of Clerics, XVII-279 pp., 1941.

131. Goodwine, Rev. John, A.B., S.T.L., J.C.D., The Right of the Church to Acquire Property, VIII-119 pp., 1941.
132. Heston, Rev. Edward Louis, C.S.C., Ph.D., S.T.D., J.C.D., The Alienation of Church Property in the United States, XII-222 pp., 1941.
133. Hogan, Rev. James John, A.B., S.T.L., J.C.D., Judicial Advocates and Procurators, XIII-200 pp., 1941.
134. Kealy, Rev. Thomas M., A.B., Litt.B., J.C.D., Dowry of Women Religious, IX-152 pp., 1941.
135. Keene, Rev. Michael James, O.S.B., J.C.D., Religious Ordinaries and Canon 198, V-164 pp., 1942.
136. Kerin, Rev. Charles A., S.S., M.A., S.T.B., J.C.D., The Privation of Christian Burial, XVI-279 pp., 1941.
137. Louis, Rev. William Francis, M.A., J.C.D., Diocesan Archives, X-101 pp., 1941.
138. McDevitt, Rev. Gilbert Joseph, A.B., J.C.D., Legitimacy and Legitimation, X-247 pp., 1941.
139. McDonough, Rev. Thomas Joseph, A.B., J.C.D., Apostolic Administrators, X-217 pp., 1941.
140. Meier, Rev. Carl Anthony, A.B., J.C.D., Penal Administrative Procedure Against Negligent Pastors, XI-240 pp., 1941.
141. Schmidt, Rev. John Rogg, A.B., J.C.D., The Principles of Authentic Interpretation in Canon 17 of the Code of Canon Law, XII-331 pp., 1941.
142. Slafkosky, Rev. Andrew Leonard, A.B., J.C.D., The Canonical Episcopal Visitation of the Diocese, X-197 pp., 1941.
143. Swoboda, Rev. Innocent Robert, O.F.M., J.C.D., Ignorance in Relation to the Imputability of Delicts, IX-271 pp., 1941.
144. Dubé, Rev. Arthur Joseph, A.B., J.C.D., The General Principles for the Reckoning of Time in Canon Law, VIII-299 pp., 1941.
145. McBride, Rev. James T., A.B., J.C.D., Incardination and Excardination of Seculars, XX-585 pp., 1941.
146. Król, Rev. John T., J.C.D., The Defendant in Ecclesiastical Trials, XII-207 pp., 1942.
147. Comyns, Rev. Joseph J., C.SS.R., A.B., J.C.D., Papal and Episcopal Administration of Church Property, XIV-155 pp., 1942.
148. Barry, Rev. Garrett Francis, O.M.I., J.C.D., Violation of the Cloister, XII-260 pp., 1942.
149. Bolduc, Rev. Gatien, C.S.V., A.B., S.T.L., J.C.D., Les Études dans les Religions Cléricales, VIII-155 pp., 1942.
150. Boyle, Rev. David John, M.A., J.C.D., The Juridic Effects of Moral Certitude on Pre-Nuptial Guarantees, XII-188 pp., 1942.
151. Canavan, Rev. Walter Joseph, M.A., Litt.D., J.C.D., The Profession of Faith, XII-143 pp., 1942.
152. Desrochers, Rev. Bruno, A.B., Ph.L., S.T.B., J.C.D., Le Premier Concile Plénier de Québec et le Code de Droit Canonique, XIV-186 pp., 1942.

153. DILLON, REV. ROBERT EDWARD, A.B., J.C.D., Common Law Marriage, X-148 pp., 1942.
154. DODWELL, REV. EDWARD JOHN, Ph.D., S.T.B., J.C.D., The Time and Place for the Celebration of Marriage, X-156 pp., 1942.
155. DONNELLAN, REV. THOMAS ANDREW, A.B., J.C.D., The Obligation of the Missa pro Populo, VII-131 pp., 1942.
156. ELTZ, REV. LOUIS ANTHONY, A.B., J.C.D., Cooperation in Crime, XII-208 pp., 1942.
157. GASS, REV. SYLVESTER FRANCIS, M.A., J.C.D., Ecclesiastical Pensions, XI-206 pp., 1942.
158. GUINIVEN, REV. JOHN JOSEPH, C.SS.R., J.C.D., The Precept of Hearing Mass, XIV-188 pp., 1942.
159. GULCZYNSKI, REV. JOHN THEOPHILUS, J.C.D., The Desecration and Violation of Churches, X-126 pp., 1942.
160. HAMMILL, REV. JOHN LEO, M.A., J.C.D., The Obligations of the Traveler According to Canon 14, VIII-204 pp., 1942.
161. HAYDT, REV. JOHN JOSEPH, A.B., J.C.D., Reserved Benefices, XI-148 pp., 1942.
162. HUSER, REV. ROGER JOHN, O.F.M., A.B., J.C.D., The Crime of Abortion in Canon Law, XII-187 pp., 1942.
163. KEARNEY, REV. FRANCIS PATRICK, A.B., S.T.L., J.C.D., The Principles of Canon 1127, X-162 pp., 1942.
164. LINAHEN, REV. LEO JAMES, S.T.L., J.C.D., De Absolutione Complicis in Peccato Turpi, V-114 pp., 1942.
165. MCCLOSKEY, REV. JOSEPH ALOYSIUS, A.B., J.C.D., The Subject of Ecclesiastical Law According to Canon 12, XVII-246 pp., 1942.
166. O'NEILL, REV. FRANCIS JOSEPH, C.SS.R., J.C.D., The Dismissal of Religious in Temporary Vows, XIII-220 pp., 1942.
167. PRINCE, REV. JOHN EDWARD, A.B., S.T.B., J.C.D., The Diocesan Chancellor, X-136 pp., 1942.
168. RIESNER, REV. ALBERT JOSEPH, C.SS.R., J.C.D., Apostates and Fugitives from Religious Institutes, IX-168 pp., 1942.
169. STENGER, REV. JOSEPH BERNARD, J.C.D., The Mortgaging of Church Property, 186 pp., 1942.
170. WALDRON, REV. JOSEPH FRANCIS, A.B., J.C.D., The Minister of Baptism, XII-197 pp., 1942.
171. WILLETT, REV. ROBERT ALBERT, J.C.D., The Probative Value of Documents in Ecclesiastical Trials, X-124 pp., 1942.
172. WOEBER, REV. EDWARD MARTIN, M.A., J.C.D., The Interpellations, XII-161 pp., 1942.
173. BENKO, REV. MATTHEW ALOYSIUS, O.S.B., M.A., J.C.D., The Abbot *Nullius*, XVI-148 pp., 1943.
174. CHRIST, REV. JOSEPH JAMES, M.A., S.T.L., J.C.D., Dispensation from Vindicative Penalties, XIV-285 pp., 1943.

175. Clancy, Rev. Patrick M. J., O.P., A.B., S.T.Lr., J.C.D., The Local Religious Superior, X-229 pp., 1943.
176. Clarke, Rev. Thomas James, J.C.D., Parish Societies, XII-147 pp., 1943.
177. Connolly, Rev. John Patrick, S.T.L., J.C.D., Synodal Examiners and Parish Priest Consultors, X-223 pp., 1943.
178. Drumm, Rev. William Martin, A.B., J.C.D., Hospital Chaplains, XII-175 pp., 1943.
179. Flanagan, Rev. Bernard Joseph, A.B., S.T.L., J.C.D., The Canonical Erection of Religious Houses, X-147 pp., 1943.
180. Kelleher, Rev. Stephen Joseph, A.B., S.T.B., J.C.D., Discussions with Non-Catholics: Canonical Legislation, X-93 pp., 1943.
181. Lewis, Rev. Gordian, C.P., J.C.D., Chapters in Religious Institutes, XII-169 pp., 1943.
182. Marx, Rev. Adolph, J.C.D., The Declaration of Nullity of Marriages Contracted Outside the Church, X-151 pp., 1943.
183. Matulenas, Rev. Raymond Anthony, O.S.B., A.B., J.C.D., Communication, a Source of Privileges, XII-225 pp., 1943.
184. O'Leary, Rev. Charles Gerard, C.SS.R., J.C.D., Religious Dismissed After Perpetual Profession, X-213 pp., 1943.
185. Power, Rev. Cornelius Michael, J.C.D., The Blessing of Cemeteries, XII-231 pp., 1943.
186. Shuhler, Rev. Ralph Vincent, O.S.A., J.C.D., Privileges of Religious to Absolve and Dispense, XII-195 pp., 1943.
187. Ziolkowski, Rev. Thaddeus Stanislaus, A.B., J.C.D., The Consecration and Blessing of Churches, XII-151 pp., 1943.
188. Heneghan, Rev. John Joseph, S.T.D., J.C.D., The Marriages of Unworthy Catholics: Canons 1065 and 1066, XVI-213 pp., 1944.
189. Carroll, Rev. Coleman Francis, M.A., S.T.L., J.C.L., Charitable Institutions.
190. Cieslук, Rev. Joseph Edward, Ph.B., S.T.L., J.C.L., National Parishes in the United States.
191. Coburn, Rev. Vincent Paul, A.B., J.C.D., Marriages of Conscience, XII-172 pp., 1944.
192. Connors, Rev. Charles Paul, C.S.Sp., A.B., J.C.D., Extra-Judicial Procurators in the Code of Canon Law, X-94 pp., 1944.
193. Coyle, Rev. Paul Raymond, A.B., J.C.D., Judicial Exceptions, X-142 pp., 1944.
194. Fair, Rev. Bartholomew Francis, A.B., S.T.L., J.C.D., The Impediment of Abduction, XII-122 pp., 1944.
195. Gallagher, Rev. Thomas Raphael, O.P., A.B., S.T.Lr., J.C.D., The Examination of the Qualities of the Ordinand, X-166 pp., 1944.
196. Gannon, Rev. John Mark, S.T.L., J.C.D., The Interstices Required for the Promotion to Orders, XII-100 pp., 1944.

197. Goldsmith, Rev. J. William, B.C.S., S.T.L., J.C.D., The Competence of Church and State Over Marriages—Disputed Points, X-128 pp., 1944.
198. Goodwine, Rev. Joseph Gerard, A.B., S.T.B., J.C.D., The Reception of Converts, XIV-326 pp., 1944.
199. Kowalski, Rev. Romuald Eugene, O.F.M., A.B., J.C.D., Sustenance of Religious Houses of Regulars, X-174 pp., 1944.
200. McCoy, Rev. Alan Edward, O.F.M., J.C.D., Force and Fear in Relation to Delictual Imputability and Penal Responsibility, XII-160 pp., 1944.
201. McDevitt, Rev. Vincent John, Ph.B., S.T.L., J.C.L., Perjury.
202. Martin, Rev. Thomas Owen, Ph.D., S.T.D., J.C.D., Adverse Possession, Prescription and Limitation of Actions: The Canonical "Praescriptio," XX-208 pp., 1944.
203. Miklosovic, Rev. Paul John, A.B., J.C.L., Attempted Marriages and Their Consequent Juridic Effects.
204. Mundy, Rev. Thomas Maurice, A.B., S.T.L., J.C.D., The Union of Parishes, X-164 pp., 1944.
205. O'Dea, Rev. John Coyle, A.B., J.C.D., The Matrimonial Impediment of Nonage, VIII-126 pp., 1944.
206. Olalia, Rev. Alexander Ayson, S.T.L., J.C.D., A Comparative Study of the Christian Constitution of States and the Constitution of the Philippine Commonwealth, XII-136 pp., 1944.
207. Poisson, Rev. Pierre-Marie, C.S.C., A.B., Ph.L., Th.L., J.C.L., Droits Patrimoniaux des Maisons et des Eglises Religieuses.
208. Stadalnikas, Rev. Casimir Joseph, M.I.C., J.C.D., Reservation of Censures, X-141 pp., 1944.
209. Sullivan, Rev. Eugene Henry, S.T.L., J.C.D., Proof of the Reception of the Sacraments, X-165 pp., 1944.
210. Vaughan, Rev. William Edward, J.C.D., Constitutions for Diocesan Courts, X-210 pp., 1944.
211. Paro, Rev. Gino, S.T.D., J.C.L., The Right of Apostolic Legation.
212. Balzer, Rev. Ralph Francis, C.P., J.C.D., The Computation of Time in a Canonical Novitiate, X-227 pp., 1945.
213. Dougherty, Rev. John Whelan, A.B., S.T.L., J.C.L., De Inquisitione Speciali.
214. Dziob, Rev. Michael Walter, J.C.L., The Sacred Congregation for the Oriental Church.
215. Eidenschink, Rev. John Albert, O.S.B., B.A., J.C.D., The Election of Bishops in the Letters of Pope Gregory the Great, VIII-200 pp., 1945.
216. Gill, Rev. Nicholas, C.P., J.C.L., The Spiritual Prefect in Clerical Religious Houses of Study.
217. Hynes, Rev. Harry Gerard, S.T.L., J.C.D., The Privileges of Cardinals, XII-183 pp., 1945.
218. McDevitt, Rev. Gerald Vincent, S.T.L., J.C.D., The Renunciation of an Ecclesiastical Office, XIV-179 pp., 1945.

219. Manning, Rev. Joseph Leroy, J.C.D., The Free Conferral of Offices, VII-116 pp., 1945.
220. Meyer, Rev. Louis G., O.S.B., A.B., S.T.B., J.C.D., Alms-gathering by Religious, XII-163 pp., 1945.
221. O'Donnell, Rev. Cletus Francis, M.A., J.C.L., The Marriage of Minors.
222. Prunskis, Rev. Joseph, J.C.D., Comparative Law, Ecclesiastical and Civil, in Lithuanian Concordat, X-161 pp., 1945.
223. Sweeney, Rev. Francis Patrick, C.SS.R., J.C.D., The Reduction of Clerics to the Lay State, X-199 pp., 1945.
224. Vogelpohl, Rev. Henry John, J.C.L., The Simple Impediments to Holy Orders.
225. Brockhaus, Rev. Thomas Aquinas, O.S.B., J.C.L., Religious who are known as *Conversi.*
226. Griese, Rev. Orville Nicholas, S.T.D., J.C.L., Marriage and the Procreation of Offspring.
227. Boudreaux, Rev. Warren Louis, J.C.L., The *"ab acatholicis nati"* of Canon 1099, § 2.
228. Bowe, Rev. Thomas Joseph, A.B., J.C.L., Religious Superioresses.
229. Diederichs, Rev. Michael Ferdinand, S.C.J., J.C.L., The Jurisdiction of the Latin Ordinaries over their Oriental Subjects.
230. Dingman, Rev. Maurice John, A.B., S.T.L., J.C.L., The Plaintiff in Contentious Trials.
231. Frison, Rev. Basil, C.M.F., M.Mus., J.C.L., The Retroactivity of Law.
232. Galvin, Rev. William Anthony, M.A., J.C.L., The Administrative Transfer of Pastors.
233. Goracy, Rev. Joseph C., J.C.L., The Diriment Matrimonial Impediment of Major Orders.
234. Hale, Rev. Joseph Francis, M.A., S.T.L., J.C.L., The Pastor of Burial.
235. Henry, Rev. Joseph Arthur, A.B., J.C.L., The Mass and Holy Communion: Interritual Law.
236. Linenberger, Rev. Herbert, C.PP.S., J.C.L., The False Denunciation of an Innocent Confessor.
237. Lowry, Rev. James Martin, A.B., J.C.L., Dispensation from Private Vows.
238. Lynch, Rev. George Edward, A.B., S.T.L., J.C.L., Coadjutors and Auxiliaries of Bishops.
239. Lynch, Rev. Timothy, M.S.SS.T., J.C.L., Contracts between Bishops and Religious Congregations.
240. McClunn, Rev. Justin David, A.B., S.T.L., J.C.L., Administrative Recourse.
241. McGarvey, Rev. Thomas Joseph, A.B., S.T.L., J.C.L., Bination.
242. McGrath, Rev. James, A.B., J.C.L., The Privilege of the Canon.
243. Marbach, Rev. Joseph Francis, A.B., J.C.L., Marriage Legislation for the Catholics of the Oriental Rites in the United States and Canada.

244. Shimkus, Rev. Bernard Aloysius, A.B., J.C.L., The Determination and Transfer of Rite.

245. Smith, Rev. Vincent Michael, A.B., S.T.L., J.C.L., Ignorance Affecting Matrimonial Consent.

246. Wachtrle, Rev. Paul Anthony, A.B., J.C.L., The Baptism of the Children of Non-Catholics.

www.ingramcontent.com/pod-product-compliance
Lightning Source LLC
LaVergne TN
LVHW050202080826
844660LV00012B/339

* 9 7 8 0 8 1 3 2 2 4 1 1 4 *